The Complete Book of Bread Machine Baking

Edited by Lara Pizzorno

PRIMA PUBLISHING

© 1997 by Trillium Health Products

PRIMA PUBLISHING and colophon are registered trademarks of Prima Communications, Inc.

Library of Congress Cataloging-in-Publication Data on file
0-7615-1125-3

97 98 99 00 01 AA 10 9 8 7 6 5 4 3 2 1
Printed in the United States of America

How to Order
Single copies may be ordered from Prima Publishing, P.O. Box 1260BK, Rocklin, CA 95677; telephone (916) 632-4400. Quantity discounts are also available. On your letterhead, include information concerning the intended use of the books and the number of books you wish to purchase.

Visit us online at www.primapublishing.com

Contents

Bread Recipes

Foreword

Bread is called "the staff of life" because it is made with grain, a highly nutritious ingredient that is relatively easy to cultivate and deliciously versatile to use.

Actually, grains have had a profound emotional, economic, and political as well as nutritional influence on our lives. For example, one-time political enemies such as the United States and the former USSR were known to have negotiated a peaceful sale of grains during times of drought. And who can deny that a sense of personal peace and emotional comfort settles over each of us when we are enjoying the scent of fresh-baked bread?

At this time in history, grains provide almost 70 percent of the diet for the majority of people in the world. Meanwhile, the earth's population continues to grow, so our reliance on grains is increasing. It is an interesting fact that although over 8,000 different species of plants supply grains, the majority of people eat only 4 of these: wheat, rice, corn, and oats. Less commonly eaten grains include rye, buckwheat, and wild rice.

We eat grains in a variety of forms, such as pancakes, breads, crackers, hot and cold breakfast cereals, cookies, cakes, and pie crusts; but what, exactly, is a grain? Most often, the term *grain* describes the seed of a member of the grass family. Edible grains are often referred to as cereal grains, referring to the Roman goddess of agriculture, Ceres.

GRAINS AND HEALTH

Although health-conscious Americans have relied on grains as a major source of fiber, vitamins, and carbohydrates for most of this century, medical authorities are now beginning to appreciate the beneficial effect of making grains a major proportion of the diet.

Diet itself is a relatively new interest of medical professionals. The National Research Council's Food and Nutrition Board (which develops the Recommended Dietary Allowances [RDAs] for desirable amounts of nutrients in daily diets) oversaw a comprehensive analysis of the relationship between diet and the development of hardening of the arteries, cancer, diabetes, arthritis, and other degenerative diseases. Their findings emphasized the urgent need for Americans to change their eating habits as a prerequisite for preventing these chronic diseases. The Surgeon General's Report on Nutrition and Health declared, "The single most influential dietary change one can make to lower the risk of these degenerative diseases is to reduce intake of foods high in fats and to increase the intake of foods high in complex carbohydrates and fiber."

Two basic facts support the inclusion of plant foods such as whole grains, legumes, fruits, and vegetables in an optimal diet: (1) a diet rich in plant food protects us against many common diseases, and (2) a diet low in plant foods is a contributing factor in the development of many diseases.

THE WAY WE WERE

Arthritis, cancer, hardening of the arteries, and other degenerative diseases are so common a part of our contemporary American lives that some of us consider them inevitable consequences of old age. Yet they all were quite rare before the turn of the twentieth century. What happened? One obvious change has been the radical alteration in our food consumption habits.

We're eating more fat and fewer carbohydrates. What is even more disturbing, over half the carbohydrates consumed by contemporary Americans are in the form of refined carbohydrates (such as white flour, white rice, sucrose, and corn syrup). Sweeteners have been linked to a long list of physical ailments common to life in twentieth-century America, such as hemorrhoids, yeast infections, hypoglycemia (low blood sugar), crankiness and poor concentration in children, and several dozen other health concerns. If you look at the ingredients on just about any commercially manufactured product made with refined grains, more than likely it is also full of fat and sugar.

WHOLE VERSUS REFINED GRAINS

Even if refined carbohydrates weren't so often linked with fat and sugar, they would still be detrimental to health. White flour is whole wheat flour that has been stripped of the vast majority of its nutrients (see Table 1). This occurs when the outer coat of the grain is removed. Thus white flour is a source of energy from carbohydrates but is not the potent source of vitamin B-complex, vitamin E, and other nutrients found in the dark-colored outer coat of the whole grain.

This outer coat of a grain is composed of anatomical structures called the bran and the germ. A volatile oil that easily spoils when exposed to heat and light is contained in this outer coat. By removing these structures, food manufacturers can significantly increase the shelf life of baked goods made from such denatured flour. The result is financial profits for the manufacturer but nutritional losses for the consumer.

You may notice heavy marketing attention focused on the word *enriched* on packages of rice, macaroni, and wheat flour. Don't be misled. First, "wheat" flour is simply refined flour. If you want the natural product with nutrients intact, look for 100% whole wheat flour. Second, as many as 20 nutrients may have been removed, while only 4 (iron, thiamin, riboflavin, and niacin) have been replaced. And this is supposed to be "enriched"!

The same sort of refining is done with other whole grains as well. For example, the majority of rice consumed in the world is eaten as white rice. White rice is produced by milling the rice to separate the outer portions of the grain (husk, bran, and aleurone) as well as the germ from the endosperm. After the husk is removed, the rice is either sold as "brown" rice or milled (polished) at least three more times to produce "white" rice. This polishing results in some nutrient loss.

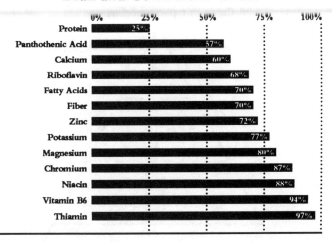

TABLE 1

Nutrient Losses Caused by Removing Bran and Germ from Wheat

Nutrient	Percent Loss
Protein	25%
Panthothenic Acid	57%
Calcium	60%
Riboflavin	68%
Fatty Acids	70%
Fiber	70%
Zinc	72%
Potassium	77%
Magnesium	80%
Chromium	87%
Niacin	88%
Vitamin B6	94%
Thiamin	97%

THE GOVERNMENT AND NUTRITION EDUCATION

Changes in food consumption patterns during this century have not gone unnoticed in government agencies, especially those whose job it is to advise American citizens about the relationship between eating habits and health. To assist Americans in choosing healthful foods each day, the U.S. Department of Agriculture (USDA) created the "Food Guide Pyramid."

At the bottom of the "Food Guide Pyramid" are grains, which the USDA tells us ought to be the foundation of our daily diet. The pyramid informs us that for optimal health we ought to eat 9 to 11 servings of whole grain breads, cereals, and pastas per day, and these servings should, according to the USDA, constitute more than half of our total dietary intake. Such is the importance of grains to good health.

FIGURE 1

Food Guide Pyramid
A Guide to Daily Food Choices

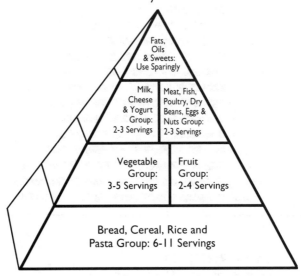

Fats,
Oils
& Sweets:
Use Sparingly

Milk,
Cheese
& Yogurt
Group:
2-3 Servings

Meat, Fish,
Poultry, Dry
Beans, Eggs &
Nuts Group:
2-3 Servings

Vegetable
Group:
3-5 Servings

Fruit
Group:
2-4 Servings

Bread, Cereal, Rice and
Pasta Group: 6-11 Servings

GRAINS: FUEL FOR CIVILIZATION

No authorities had to encourage our ancestors to eat more grains. Grains were among the first cultivated crops. Wheat and barley, for example, were grown over 10,000 years ago in the Middle East. Other areas of the world took up grain farming a bit later. By 4000 B.C., millet farming was well established along the upper Yellow River in China, and about the same time rice was being cultivated elsewhere in Southeast Asia.

As people traveled, they took their grain stores with them. In fact, archeologists believe that the cultivation of grains and the development of grain-based foods such as bread contributed greatly to the spread of civilization.

Some experts believe that grains are an answer to the global population explosion that threatens the stability of humankind in our own day, for in addition to their numerous health benefits, grains and other plant foods offer the only sustainable solution to world hunger.

Grains, for example, provide substantially more available food energy per acre than livestock. To produce just 1 pound of beef, 16 pounds of grain and soy must be used. What is more, if Americans reduced their consumption of meat by just 10 percent (not eating 1 hamburger for every 9 eaten), 100 million people could be adequately nourished using the land, water, and energy freed from growing fodder for the animal that would have created that 10th hamburger patty.*

THE EASY WAY TO ADD GRAIN TO OUR DIET

For busy, health-conscious Americans, the difficulty has been finding the time to prepare nutritious whole grains. Fortunately, with the advent of the automatic bread machine, this has never been easier to do. With recipes developed by nutritionists, we can begin now to include more whole grains in our diet and turn back the nutritional clock to a healthier time.

* Robbins, John. *Diet for a New America*. NH: Stillpoint Press, 1987.

A Note To Readers

Substituting Unbleached Flour for Whole Wheat Flour

A hallmark of whole grain bread is its natural denseness. If you find that you prefer a loaf with a more familiar taste and texture, replace up to half the amount of whole wheat flour of any recipe with unbleached flour. The nutritional analysis at the end of each recipe is for a loaf made according to the directions. If you change the proportion of whole grain to unbleached flour in any recipe, the nutritional analysis will change as well.

Also, please check your machine instruction booklet to make sure your machine can bake whole wheat breads. There are a few machines on the market today equipped to make only lighter, white breads. If you bake whole grain breads in this type of machine, you'll eventually wear down the motor.

Acknowledgments

Just as a perfect loaf of bread develops from the synergistic melding of a variety of ingredients, so has this book emerged from the combined talents of many gifted individuals.

SPECIAL THANKS ARE DUE:

To Frances Albrecht, Kristen Wade, Barbara Heathcote, Brenda Wolsey, and Daniella Chace, for their research and recipes.

To Barbara Heathcote, Frances Albrecht, Lara Pizzorno, and Michael Murray—for writing the text accompanying each recipe.

To Gerald Koblentz, for his expert troubleshooting advice.

To our recipe tester, Suzanne Levine, and to bread baking genius Sam Nassar, whose alchemy transformed problem loaves into perfection.

To Carolyn Reuben, for carefully crafting our words.

To everyone at Prima, especially Ben Dominitz, Jennifer Basye, Andi Reese Brady, and Becky Freeman, for patiently waiting until every recipe rose to our highest expectations.

And to you, our readers, whose desire for good health as well as great taste inspired us to create these wonderful, nourishing breads.

CHAPTER ONE

Choosing a Bread Machine

bread baking machine is a major investment, not only financially, but also emotionally. If you are like most bread machine owners, you aren't going to hide the machine in a distant cupboard with equipment you rarely use. After you have baked your first 6 loaves, you will have worked out the most common problems encountered in bread baking by machine and will have achieved some perfect loaves. You will most likely discover that you and your family now expect fresh bread every morning. As a result, you and your bread machine are going to have a lasting relationship. Thus you had better take the time to choose a machine you're going to like working with even when you're tired, impatient, grumpy, and, of course, busy.

In addition to asking store personnel for advice, make sure you are given the chance to touch test (opening the lid, pulling out the bread pan with your hand in a thick mitt, setting the timer, and so on). Ask your relatives, friends, and acquaintances for their experiences with their own bread machines. When you comparison shop, look for four major characteristics: quality, design, convenience, and consumer education.

QUALITY

To what extent does the company stand behind its product? Is there an adequate customer service team to answer your questions when problems arise while you are baking bread?

What kind of warranty does the machine have? Bread machine warranties normally range anywhere from 3 months to 1 year. The best value is probably the one with a company behind it that believes their machine is durable enough to last for at least a year.

DESIGN

Your machine's design can make all the difference in the world. The proper design will allow you the freedom to make almost any type of bread you choose.

Horsepower/Power

Some machines have a more difficult time handling 100% whole grains because such grains make heavier loaves than refined flour. If you expect to bake mostly with whole grains, look for a machine with increased horsepower to more easily handle the heavier, healthier, whole grain flour. Most newer machines can handle heavy dough. Still, it's a good idea to listen to your machine as it kneads heavier breads. If it sounds as though it is straining add a little more liquid.

Bread Pan

Bread pans come in many different sizes and shapes. Machines produce oblong, round, rectangular and square loaves. If you want to make bread for one primary use, say sandwiches, the shape of the pan will make a difference. Make sure the machine you choose produces the right shape for your needs.

Domes or Windows

We prefer a machine with a window rather than a dome. First, and most important, some dome machines lose heat out of the top. Also, it's good to be able to check the bread, especially when experimenting with new recipes, to see if it appears too wet or dry during the kneading, to prevent overflows, or to spot a loaf that fails to rise.

CONVENIENCE

Timer

Make sure the timer is easy to use. Test out different models and brands in the store. Avoid any timer that is the least bit confusing!

Cycles

Extra cycles on some machines enable you to create jams and quick breads. These cycles are convenient features for specialty uses, and you should consider what types of breads you will be making when you select your machine. For example, if your family prefers sweet breads you may want to choose a machine with this cycle, although sweet breads may be made in any machine (your owner's manual can help you adapt time and temperatures if you do not have a cycle for the type of bread you want to bake).

- Preheat. With this feature you don't need to spend time bringing your ingredients to room temperature, the machine does it for you.

- Basic. This is the all-purpose cycle used for most breads. You can use it, adapting as directed by your owner's manual, for almost any type of baking.

- Quick. This cycle cuts cooking time by about an hour. Some machines are programmed as rapid bake—their regular cycle is as short as 2 1/2 hours, making all of their breads rapid bake.

- Whole Wheat or Whole Grain. This cycle provides the longer rising times needed for heavier breads. With some machines you may need to make adjustments if you don't have this cycle or have the option of programming longer kneading and baking times. You can stop and restart your machine after the first kneading cycle, if necessary. Check the owner's manual if you're not sure.

- French Bread. Lowers the amount of kneading time and increases the time for rising. For recipes that are low in fat and sugar. This cycle makes bread with a crisp crust.
- Dough/Manual. Use this cycle to mix and knead the dough, and allow it to rise. You may then enjoy shaping the dough with your hands and baking it in a conventional oven.
- Raisin/Nut. This is really a timer that signals when to add the fruit or nuts so they are not smashed, or dried out, before the baking begins.
- Bake-Only. This cycle is good for baking frozen doughs, although most of what a bake-only cycle does can be done in a conventional oven.
- Sweet Bread. Sugar affects the rising time and baking temperature, and this cycle compensates. Check your owner's manual for when to use this cycle or for adapting a machine without this cycle when making sweet bread.
- Timed-Bake. How convenient to wake up or come home from work to fresh baked bread. However, do not use this cycle with recipes that include eggs, milk and other perishables, since they can spoil. (You may substitute dry milk powder for recipes calling for milk. Equivalents are shown on dry milk packages, however baking times is usually 4 hours instead of 3. Check your manual—a few machines, including Black & Decker, have a powdered milk setting).
- Cool-Down/Keep-Warm. To prevent soggy bread caused by condensation, remove the loaf as soon as it is done baking. For those times when you cannot be present to remove the bread at the right time, a cool-down cycle allows the bread to remain in the

machine with minimum condensation. If the machine doesn't have a cool-down cycle it probably has a keep-warm cycle instead, which will keep your loaf warm for up to an hour.

EDUCATION

Read the instructional booklet that comes with the machine. What you want are educational materials that are clear and precise and enable you to bake breads that consistently rise to your expectations.

Look for:

- an **instruction manual** that thoroughly covers the use and care of the machine, including what to do when machine parts become clogged or dysfunctional and who to call for advice or repairs.

- a **video** that visually teaches you to use the machine properly, fine tunes your measuring skills, and inspires your creativity.

- a **recipe book** with recipes that consistently work in your machine. The more recipes you're comfortable with, the more flexibility you'll have in creating consistently delicious and varied loaves for years to come.

BREAD MACHINE MANUFACTURERS

The following bread machines can be used to create the recipes in this book: American Harvest, Aroma, Betty Crocker, Black & Decker, Decosonic, Hitatchi, MK Seiko, Mr. Coffee, Panasonic/National, Pillsbury, Proctor-Silex, Red Star, Regal, Salton/Maxim, Sanyo, Sunbeam-Oster, Toastmaster, Welbilt, West Bend, Williams Sonoma, and Zojirushi.

Specialty Cycles.

Some machines have features available from only one, or just a few, manufacturers.

- Jam. Allows you to make your own jam. (Aroma, Hitachi, Zojirushi.)

- Rice. Cook rice in your bread machine. (Aroma, Hitachi.)
- Roast. Cook chicken, roasts. (Aroma.)
- Butter. Whip your butter, with recipes. (Toastmaster.)
- Cake. Make sweet breads and non-yeast breads such as banana-nut bread. (Aroma, Betty Crocker, Black & Decker, Hitachi, West Bend, Williams Sonoma, Panasonic, MK Seiko, Zojirushi.)
- Yogurt. Instructions on making yogurt in the machine. (Aroma.)
- Pasta. Kneads the dough—you roll it out. (Williams Sonoma).
- Pizza Dough. Makes two sizes. (Hitachi.)
- Cookie Dough, Pastry Dough. (Williams Sonoma, MK Seiko, Welbilt.)
- Specialty. Allows you to remove the dough and stuff it, then place it back in the machine for rising or cooking. (Panasonic.)

Size of Bread Pan

Bread pans range from 1 pound to 2 pounds. The larger pan is the better buy. After all, you can always bake a 1-pound loaf in the larger pan.

Crust Color Selection

This feature allows you to control the brownness of the crust. Caution: With some machines a lighter setting can result in breads that are gummy on top, especially sweet breads.

Power Saver

The power saver is a memory device that saves your bread in the event of power interruption, such as an inadvertent pulling of a plug or temporary loss of power. The power saver in some machines gives you just 10 seconds to restore power, in others it gives you up to 10 minutes. If power is restored within the set time the baking process will continue where it left off.

CHAPTER TWO

Quality Ingredients:

The Key to Distinctively Delicious Breads

Tired of the same old basics from the bread aisle in your supermarket? With just a little imagination and your bread machine, you can bake a different bread every day of the year. Just change or add an ingredient, and each loaf of healthy, homemade bread will take on a whole new look, taste, texture, and appeal.

What do we suggest for distinctively delicious breads? Ingredient possibilities are as wide ranging as the foods in your refrigerator or the herbs and spices on your pantry shelf. Let's start with the basics — flour, yeast, water, a drop of sweetener, and a dash of salt — that enable you to make most bread recipes, whether in your bread machine or by hand. Even among these basic ingredients, modern bread bakers can be faced with a confusing array of products. The information in this chapter will teach you how to become an expert in selecting and storing the best basic ingredients — particularly whole grain flours. These flours will make a substantial difference in both the taste and nutritional quality of your breads.

Flour

Until recently, the myth that white flour is as nutritious as whole wheat flour misled many nutrition-conscious consumers. Today, however, we know that whole wheat or other whole grain flours are nutritionally superior to refined flours; whole grains contain more vitamins, minerals, protein, complex carbohydrates, essential oils, and fiber. Whole grain breads are not only far more nutritious, they also provide richer flavors and heartier textures. To gradually acquaint you with the delights of whole grain breads, many of the recipes call for a mix of whole wheat flour and unbleached flour. The resulting breads are more nutritious than the typical store-bought bread but retain a familiar lighter texture and taste.

When you purchase wheat flour, be certain to purchase *whole* wheat flour, not just wheat flour, as the latter has been refined. Also, look for flour that has been stone-milled. Although slightly harder to find, flour made by slow, cool grinding with stone mills offers the highest quality, both in nutrients and taste. Today, most flour milling is done by high-speed, high-volume steel cylinders or hammer mills. These mills grind with ridged or smooth pairs of cylinders that rotate at high speed and generate a great deal of heat. At 119°F, most of the healthful live enzymes in the flour are destroyed. At higher temperatures, many other nutrients are lost. Cylinder mills heat grains to 150°F, but stone mills grind grains at temperatures below 90°F. Cylinder milling also greatly increases the flour's exposure to air, resulting in increased oxidation and rancidity of the oils in the flour. The end product is a flour that quickly spoils, losing its freshness, flavor, and aroma. Hammer mills, the most widely used commercial mills today, run at ultra-high speeds and are hotter and faster than cylinder mills. These mills produce a flour even more depleted of nutrients and flavor.

The refined flour produced by cylinder and hammer mills is subjected to further adulteration by chemicals used to age, bleach, and whiten it and to extend its shelf life. Additives routinely used include: *chlorine dioxide* (an irritant to both skin and respiratory tract used as a bleaching agent), *benzoyl peroxide* (a skin irritant also used as a bleaching agent), *methyl bromide, nitrogen trichloride, alum, chalk, nitrogen peroxide,* and *ammonium carbonate.* As you might expect, such processing lessens not only nutrients but also flavor. The flavor of refined flours is a pale reflection of the wonderful, rich taste of the original grains. Don't just take our word for it — try using fresh whole grain flours in your breads. You won't believe the difference in flavor and appetite satisfaction you'll receive from whole grain breads. Remember, though, that whole grain flour should be used within a few weeks or stored in your freezer to maintain its freshness.

Because wheat's high gluten content makes it the ideal flour for leavened bread, it is the whole grain flour most often used in the recipes provided in this book. (Gluten is a protein contained in highest amounts in the endosperm of wheat.) During the kneading and baking process, gluten expands, forming elastic strands that trap the gas released by the yeast, which causes the bread to rise. Wheat flour is classified as either hard or soft, depending on its protein content. Wheat flour used for baking bread should be hard, preferably with a protein (gluten) content of 14 percent or higher. Of the different varieties of wheat, both hard red winter wheat and hard red spring wheat typically contain this percentage of protein. Wheat flour made from soft red winter wheat or white wheat, as is typically the case in pastry flour, has less protein and should only be used for baking cakes and pastries. This is why pastry flour, even whole wheat pastry flour, is too low in gluten to produce a proper rise. Do not use pastry flour for baking bread.

Bran

The bran, the outer layer of the grain, provides most of the fiber and some vitamins and minerals. Research studies suggest that fiber reduces the risk of diverticulosis, colon and rectal cancer, and atherosclerosis. Diets with adequate fiber inherently tend to be lower in calories and fats, especially saturated fats and cholesterol. That might be one reason high-fiber diets reduce the risk of these diseases. More fiber is also good for your waistline because you'll feel fuller with fewer calories.

Both the United States Department of Agriculture (USDA) and the Department of Social and Health Services (DSHS) recommend eating a diet rich in fiber. Although the USDA recommends between 20 and 30 grams of fiber a day and the National Cancer Institute recommends 25 to 35 grams, the worldwide average intake of fiber ranges between 40 and 60 grams daily. In parts of Africa, Central and South America, daily fiber intake is 80 to 90 grams a day! Unfortunately, most Americans consume a mere 10 to 15 grams of fiber per day. With your bread machine, you'll find it's easy to improve your fiber intake by making delicious whole grain breads a staple part of your meals and snacks.

Germ

The germ is the *heart of the grain*. Although it accounts for only 2.5 percent of the kernel's weight, the germ provides the majority of the grain's important nutrients, including most of its B complex vitamins, vitamin E, calcium, iron, magnesium, and zinc. Because the essential oils contained in the germ turn rancid quickly unless whole grain flour is stored in the freezer, the germ is often removed for commercial baking. The resulting refined flour has an extended shelf life, but its nutrient value is greatly depleted. For a substantial nutrient boost and a delicious nutty flavor, try adding wheat germ to your bread recipes, even those made with whole grain flours. Be sure to buy wheat germ in vacuum-packed bottles and store it in your freezer to preserve freshness. Not sure if the wheat germ is still fresh? Smell it. If wheat germ doesn't smell sweet and nutty, discard it.

Endosperm

The endosperm is the starchy part of the grain and is all that remains after refining. This refined, endosperm-rich product is what is used to produce white flour, the flour most commonly used in commercially baked goods such as bread, rolls, muffins, and cakes. Although the endosperm accounts for about 83 percent of the kernel weight and the greatest share of the grain's protein, it lacks fiber, zinc, vitamin B6, magnesium, potassium, vitamin E, and chromium. These naturally occurring nutrients all play important roles in maintaining health, including the proper digestion and utilization of wheat or any other grain. Chromium, for example, assists insulin in taking sugar from the blood to use for energy. Without this natural balance, refined flour acts much like refined sugar in the body, disrupting blood sugar levels while providing little long-term energy.

YEAST

The dry active yeast used in baking as a leavening agent is actually a living, though dormant, single-celled organism. When exposed to warm water and sugar, the yeast revives, rapidly dividing, multiplying, and giving off carbon dioxide in the process. It is this carbon dioxide by-product that becomes trapped in the flour's gluten strands and causes the bread to rise.

The two most readily available brands of active dry yeast are Red Star® and Fleischmann's®. These can be found in sealed packets, usually in the refrigerator sections of most grocery stores. Each packet contains about 2³/₄ teaspoons of yeast. While some bakers swear by Red Star, others prefer Fleischmann's. We've had the best results with Red Star, but we recommend you try both to see which you prefer. Do *not,* however, use the following: nutritional yeast, such as torula or brewer's yeast (these are inactive), or compressed yeast or rapid rise yeast (neither gives good results in bread machines).

It is important that your yeast be fresh. To ensure freshness, only buy yeast kept in the grocer's refrigerator case, and store it in your refrigerator at home. Yeast should remain fresh for about 3 months. If your loaves aren't rising as high as expected, test or *proof* your yeast by adding 1 teaspoon of yeast and 1 tablespoon of honey to 1 cup of warm water (about 110°F, 43°C). If the mixture doesn't begin to bubble and foam in a few minutes, throw it out with the rest of your old yeast and buy some fresh packets.

Sweetener

A small amount of sweetener provides food for the yeast and, depending on which sweetener you choose, can add delicious, home-baked flavor to your bread. Most recipes in this book use honey because it provides a smooth, rich flavor; and because honey tastes almost twice as sweet as sugar, you get the same sweetening effect with half the amount. Molasses, especially unsulfured blackstrap molasses, is undoubtedly the most nutritious sweetener and is a wonderful choice for rich, spicy breads such as a gingerbread loaf. In less flavorful breads, however, its strong flavor may be overpowering. For those who prefer a less distinctive flavor than honey or molasses, maple syrup offers a natural alternative with a milder taste. Be certain to use *pure* maple syrup, not the less expensive maple-flavored corn syrups that usually contain less than 3 percent real maple syrup. Store maple syrup in your refrigerator to ensure lasting freshness.

Liquid

Liquid provides the medium for dissolving the yeast and combining ingredients to form a kneadable, elastic dough. Fresh, clear, warm water (around 80 – 90°F or 26.7 – 32.2°C — much hotter and it will kill the yeast, colder and the yeast will work too slowly) is the most frequent choice, but soy milk, rice milk, cow's milk, buttermilk, or fresh vegetable or fruit juice can also be substituted in an equal amount for additional nutrients and flavor.

CREATING DISTINCTIVE BREADS

What's homemade bread without a little character? In *The Complete Book of Bread Machine Baking,* you'll find recipes so varied you can bake a new and unique bread every day of the year. Sooner or later, however, you'll probably get the urge to try your hand at creating your own recipes. When the mood strikes, take a look at the following suggestions.

Herbs and Spices

Nothing tastes better with hearty soups and stews than savory herb rolls or a slice of fragrant, spiced bread. Seasoned breads are truly easy to make and fun to experiment with because of the diverse array of herbs and spices available. Be forewarned — when it comes to flavor, a little spice goes a long way.

Several factors affect the strength and flavor of herbs and spices. Drying concentrates the flavor of herbs, so if you use fresh herbs, use *half* of what is called for. If you have an herb garden or purchase fresh herbs, you can lightly toast them on a cookie sheet in the oven (250°F), until lightly toasted, then grind herbs in a coffee grinder or blender. To prolong your herb's freshness, grind only the amount you'll need for your recipe and keep the remainder in its whole form.

The following herbs and spices are tried and true additions for breads, but feel free to experiment — any herb or spice you and your family enjoy can add a special touch to your bread. Depending on whether you prefer lightly or highly seasoned foods, you can add as little as 1 teaspoon or as much as 2 tablespoons of a dried herb. (Remember, when using *fresh* herbs, use twice as much—from 2 teaspoons for lightly seasoned bread to 4 tablespoons for strongly flavored bread.)

Basil	Marjoram
Caraway	Mustard
Cardamon	Nutmeg
Cilantro	Oregano
Cinnamon	Pepper
Cumin	Rosemary
Dill	Tarragon
Fennel	Thyme

Salt

Salt is an important ingredient in bread baking. It strengthens the structure of the loaf, preventing the cooked dough from caving in. Salt also controls the rate at which yeast multiplies. The percentage of salt in a normal loaf will equal approximately $1^1/_2$ to $2^1/_2$ percent of the weight of the flour.

Nuts and Seeds

With your bread machine you can create some truly exceptional — and healthful — nut and seed breads not available anywhere else. Remember the adage, "From little acorns, big oaks grow"? Nuts and seeds are real nutritional powerhouses, providing essential fats and proteins in a deliciously snackable form. Nuts and seeds are also an excellent source of several important nutrients, including calcium, phosphorus, magnesium, and potassium. Just $1/2$ cup of sunflower seeds provides you with 50 percent of your daily potassium requirements — more than 3 times the amount of potassium found in a banana. In addition, when you bake breads, you can be selective in your choice of ingredients, choosing only nuts and seeds that you know are not rancid, and choosing more exotic nuts such as macadamia nuts, hazelnuts, chestnuts, or black walnuts for a special festive touch. Your delicious nut and seed breads will have a crunchy texture, perfect for toasting, topping with fruit conserves, or making a hearty sandwich. To avoid rancidity look for nuts still in their shells. Unshelled nuts will keep indefinitely in any cool, dry place. If you buy exposed nutmeats, purchase these from a refrigerator or freezer case or in vacuum-packed containers. Store shelled nuts in your freezer for maximum freshness.

Cheese and Yogurt

Dairy products are used in some bread recipes to add height, lightness, tenderness, flavor, color, and nutrition. Although these ingredients have traditionally been used in homemade bread, dairy products are generally high in saturated fat, so we provide health-conscious alternatives.

Cheese in the form of cottage cheese, hard cheese, or yogurt is used in many bread recipes for added flavor, taste, and protein. Cottage cheese boosts the loaf's protein content. Try to use a 1-percent fat cottage cheese. Hard cheeses make delectable corn breads and vegetable muffins, but they can raise the fat content considerably. Choose lowfat cheeses, or use smaller amounts of full-flavor cheeses like sharp cheddar. Cheese often combines well with herbs and spices in recipes for rolls, muffins, and loaves; but when you add cheese, be sure to lessen the amount of liquid used in your recipe. Typically, 3 ounces of grated cheddar or a similar hard cheese requires a decrease of 1 ounce of liquid. Fresh yogurt gives bread a tanginess not available from other ingredients and is available in a nonfat version.

CONVERTING A RECIPE

Anytime you try a new recipe it's important to keep an eye on your bread, since you may have to adjust. Frequently, manufacturers include tips for converting a recipe in their manuals. When converting a recipe:

- add the ingredients in the order specified in your owner's manual.

- make sure the flour matches your bread pan: 2 cups for a 1-pound loaf, 3 cups for a 1 1/2-pound loaf, and 4 cups for a 2-pound loaf. If the recipe uses more than 1 type of flour remember to adapt accordingly, so that the total amount of flour does not exceed the size of your pan.

- adjust the yeast to 3/4 teaspoon for a 1-pound loaf, 1 teaspoon for a 1 1/2-pound loaf, or 1 1/4 teaspoon for a 2 pound loaf.

- adjust your other ingredients proportionately. If you have reduced the flour by one-quarter, reduce the other ingredients by the same amount.

- add special ingredients, such as fruit, before shaping the loaf by hand.

- add gluten flour (1 to 3 tablespoons) if using all-purpose flour. Better yet, use bread flour.

- use the cycle that matches the ingredients. For breads with sugar or other sweeteners use the sweet bread cycle and the light-crust setting. For breads made with whole wheat or rye flour, use the whole grain cycle or follow the manufacturer's instructions.

CHAPTER THREE

Troubleshooting

Make a point of looking at your dough several times during its creation. After looking at several batches, you'll learn what the proper consistency should be for a perfect loaf. Briefly lifting the lid of your bread machine to check on your bread's progress will not affect the dough's development and may prevent a failed loaf.

Your dough should form into a slightly elastic ball 3 to 8 minutes into the kneading cycle. If your dough doesn't look quite right, review this chapter to find your problem and the possible solutions. Even if your breads are consistently delicious, read through this section. You'll gain a better understanding of the intricacies of the bread baking process.

OVERLY MOIST DOUGH

Dough appears wet and soggy. Typically this results when too many moist ingredients are added.

Problem: Too much liquid

Solution: Be sure to adjust the water accordingly when you add moist ingredients such as yogurt, applesauce, canned or fresh fruit, and vegetables. Try to estimate the amount of water in the ingredient and reduce the water in the recipe by the same amount. Or you can try adding more flour to absorb the excess moisture. Add flour, 1 tablespoon at a time, allowing enough time for flour to work its way in before adding additional flour.

OVERLY DRY DOUGH

Dough separates or crumbles rather than forming a ball. The ingredients did not mix well. Usually this is due to not enough water. Wait 4 to 5 minutes into the mixing cycle before you decide your dough is too dry; perfectly made dough often appears dry and crumbly during the first few minutes but will soon form a ball.

Problem: Too little liquid

Solution: Add water 1 tablespoon at a time, allowing enough time for water to mix in before you add additional water.

MUSHROOM LOAVES

This loaf might taste good, but it looks like a mushroom. It can also stick to the top of your machine. If you're confronted with a mushroom loaf, you have added 1 of the following:

Problem: Too much yeast

Solution: Remember, yeast is usually measured in teaspoons, not tablespoons. Typically, a $1^1/2$-pound loaf includes $1^1/2$ to $2^1/2$ teaspoons of regular active dry yeast.

Problem: Too much sweetener or ingredients containing natural sugar (e.g., dried fruit)

Solution: Sugar feeds the yeast. Too much sugar can cause the bread to rise too high. Most successful bread recipes include from 1 to 4 tablespoons of sweetener.

Problem: Too much liquid

Solution: Try decreasing the liquid 1 tablespoon at a time. If you are converting a recipe that uses sugar to one that uses honey or molasses, for every 5 teaspoons of sweetener, use 1 teaspoon less water.

SKYSCRAPER LOAVES

Similar to the mushroom, the skyscraper loaf rises too high and often sticks to the top of the machine. Usually, this occurs because you have used either too large a quantity of ingredients, too large a proportion of gluten (if gluten is among your dry ingredients), or too much yeast.

Problem: Too great a quantity of ingredients

Solution: If your bread's texture and taste are good, then your recipe is just too large overall. Try reducing the amount of all ingredients by 25 percent.

Problem: Too much gluten

Solution: If this is your error, your bread will have a chewy texture, and the top of your loaf won't mushroom out much but will go straight up. Try reducing the amount of gluten by 50 percent.

Problem: Too much yeast

Solution: If your loaf is too airy and has an overly fluffy texture, you've used too much yeast. A typical store-bought package of yeast contains 7 grams. You generally want to use between 4 and 7 grams of regular active dry yeast.

CRATER LOAVES

This loaf rises well but falls in the center as it bakes. It ends up looking like Mount Saint Helens. Crater loaves typically occur because of too much moisture or lack of salt.

Problem: Too much moisture

Solution: If the top or sides cave in, you probably used too much liquid. Try reducing the water about 2 tablespoons at a time. If you are using fresh or canned fruits or vegetables as ingredients, remember to lessen the amount of water in your recipe to account for their liquid content. Cheese breads, which have a higher moisture level because of the moisture in cheese, also have a tendency to fall in the center. Try reducing the water between 1 tablespoon and $1/4$ cup, depending on the moistness of your bread.

Problem: Lack of salt

Solution: Salt strengthens the structure of bread. If the bread lacks enough salt, it's likely to cave in or be flat on top. A $1^1/2$-pound loaf typically has 1 to $1^1/2$ teaspoons of salt. If you're already using $1^1/2$ teaspoons, then lack of salt is not your problem. If you're using only 1 teaspoon, add a bit more.

SQUAT LOAVES

This loaf may be caved in slightly, but its main problem is a lack of height. Squat loaves don't appear to have risen high enough. This may be caused by heavier ingredients, coarsely ground grains, insufficient or stale yeast, insufficient water, or water that is too cold.

Problem: Heavier ingredients

Solution: Sometimes breads made with ingredients such as nuts, dried fruit, or heartier flours such as oat, whole wheat, kasha, or cracked wheat will not rise as high (or will cave in slightly) because the structure provided by the gluten cannot sustain the extra weight. This might be fine. Taste your bread; you might have a delicious but dense loaf. Some breads taste even better when dense.

Problem: Coarsely ground wheat

Solution: Coarsely ground wheat can break apart the network of gluten strands that develops when the dough is kneaded, which causes damage to the structure of the loaf. Either decrease the amount of coarsely ground wheat used or substitute a more finely ground grain.

Problem: Insufficient or stale yeast

Solution: Be sure you're using at least 4 grams of yeast but no more than 7. Check the expiration date: if your yeast is old, it will not work as effectively. Also remember that yeast should be stored in a cool, dry place. Poor storage conditions will shorten its life span.

Problem: Insufficient water

Solution: The amount of water you use should equal approximately 60 to 70 percent of the combined weight of the flour and gluten used, particularly if the bread you are baking is composed primarily of wheat. Too little water can result in a dry, squat loaf. Paradoxically, even though a squat loaf can appear doughy inside, it also can be lacking adequate water. Sufficient water is necessary for the gluten to develop and to make the dough pliable enough to rise. If too little water is used, the dough will not rise enough for the heat to bake it thoroughly, causing the finished loaf to be too wet inside.

Problem: Water that is too cold

Solution: The temperature of water is often overlooked by new bread bakers. Yeast activates best when the water is no cooler than tepid (about 85°F, 30°C). If the water in your tap feels cool to the touch on the day you're baking, warm it to the point where you don't feel drops of it on your arm.

CRUMBLY LOAVES

This loaf is very dry and crumbles when sliced. Dry, crumbly bread is probably caused by too little liquid or fat. Bread made with 100% whole grain naturally tends to be drier and more dense than breads made with refined flour. These breads need a little extra liquid or fat.

Problem: Too little liquid

Solution: For most breads, water should equal 60 to 70 percent of the combined weight of the flour and gluten. If your recipe calls for juice or other wet ingredients, such as applesauce, try to estimate how much water is in these ingredients and adjust your recipe accordingly. If the area in which you live generally has a low humidity or if the weather on the day you are baking is dry, try adding an extra 1 to 2 tablespoons of water.

Problem: Too little fat

Solution: If there is no fat in your recipe, try adding 1 to 3 tablespoons of oil or butter.

DOUGHY LOAVES

This bread appears normal, but when you slice it, it is doughy or gooey in the center. The most common reason for this symptom is that the bread did not cook long enough. This typically happens with heavy flours such as whole wheat because these ingredients are more dense. Alternately, the dough can have too little yeast, too much water, or even too little water.

Problem: Insufficient cooking time

Solution: Try setting your bread machine on a cycle with a longer baking time, or try a cycle that has an extra knead, which will put more air in the dough and allow it to cook more quickly.

Problem: Too little yeast

Solution: Insufficient yeast prevents the dough from rising adequately. The heat cannot penetrate properly, so the dough remains too moist inside.

Problem: Too much or too little water

Solution: If too much water has been used, the water will not evaporate during the baking cycle, so you will be left with a doughy loaf. If too little water has been used, the dough will not be kneaded properly, so the dough will rise insufficiently, the heat will not penetrate to dry it out, and you will be once again left with a doughy loaf. If your recipe calls for 3 cups of flour, then you should be using approximately 10 to 11 ounces of water. Remember, when you use a liquid sweetener such as honey, or moist ingredients such as fruit and vegetables, you need to decrease the amount of water used. If you use dry ingredients such as bran or dried fruits that absorb water, you must increase the amount of water used accordingly.

GNARLY LOAVES

This loaf will be twisted and misshapen — probably short and compressed. If your bread is gnarled and twisted and doesn't rise properly, this is almost always due to too little liquid. Without enough liquid, the dough cannot be kneaded properly. To be sure, check the dough right before it begins to bake. If the loaf is compressed and gnarled, you have too little liquid. Try reducing the flour or increasing the liquid until you reach the right dough consistency. If the loaf appears normal right before baking, refer to the Crater Loaves instructions.

Problem: Too little liquid

Solution: Try increasing the liquid 1 tablespoon at a time.

Problem: Too much flour

Solution: Try reducing the flour 1/8 cup or 2 tablespoons at a time.

HOCKEY PUCK LOAVES

This loaf is hard and flat and resembles a slightly squared-off hockey puck. You probably forgot the yeast or used yeast that was inactive.

Problem: No yeast or inactive yeast

Solution: If your bread is flat, short, and hard, test the yeast. In a 1-cup measuring cup, dissolve 1 teaspoon of honey or granulated sugar and 1 tablespoon (about 1 packet) of yeast in 1/2 cup of warm water. Stir the yeast. In 3 to 4 minutes, the yeast will have absorbed enough liquid to activate and start rising to the surface. If after 10 minutes the yeast has multiplied to the 1-cup mark and has a rounded crown, it is active. You can use this yeast mixture in your next dough, but remember to deduct the 1/2 cup of liquid from the total liquid used in the recipe.

Problem: Water too hot or too cool

Solution: Ideally, water should be slightly warm (about 85°F, 30°C). Improper water temperature inhibits the yeast. If it's too hot, it kills the yeast; if too cold, the yeast remains inactive.

Problem: Too much salt

Solution: Salt controls the rate at which yeast multiplies. Typically, the percentage of salt should be between 1 1/2 and 2 1/2 percent of the weight of the flour. For a loaf made with 3 cups of flour, approximately 1 1/2 teaspoons of salt should be used. Make sure you are measuring your salt with a teaspoon, not a tablespoon.

SOGGY CRUST

The outside of the bread feels squishy and looks wrinkled. This is usually due to improper cooling.

Problem: Too little time cooling

Solution: Be certain to allow your bread to cool sufficiently. Typically, let the bread cool at least 20 to 30 minutes on a wire rack before slicing. Bread must be completely cooled, usually an hour or more, before you store it in plastic bags or other containers.

Problem: Condensation

Solution: It is best to remove the bread from your bread machine and bread pan almost immediately after it finishes baking. Leaving the bread in the machine or in the pan can lead to soggy crusts because water continues to evaporate from the hot finished loaf and condenses on bread still encased in the pan.

CRACKED LOAVES

This loaf's top is cracked and broken. In terms of taste, this is not really a problem. Even though your loaf doesn't look perfect, it will probably taste great. Even the best bakers can't always prevent this. Adding some oil may help.

FINISHED LOAVES VARY IN HEIGHT

This can be the result of using different flours, baking at different altitudes, or baking in different weather conditions. Small measuring differences in the amount of water or in the activity of the yeast can also affect the height of the loaf.

Problem: Different flours

Solution: Different flours rise to different heights. Different grains vary in rising potential. No other grain rises as well as wheat. Refined wheat flour will, as a rule, rise higher than whole wheat flour. There are also significant variations between one batch of whole wheat flour and another. The most critical element is the amount of gluten—the protein in wheat. Look for whole wheat flour, commonly called bread flour, that is high in gluten. Do not use pastry flour, even whole wheat pastry flour, because it is too low in gluten to produce a risen loaf.

Problem: Altitude

Solution: If you live at a higher elevation, your loaves can rise well but then crash during baking. The low air pressure at higher altitudes creates less resistance for the yeast, so the yeast causes the dough to rise too high, and the gluten structure cannot support the height of the loaf. Reduce your yeast by 1/2 teaspoon at a time until you reach the perfect balance for your location and machine.

Problem: Climate conditions

Solution: Humidity, temperature, and water quality can all affect your bread results. Yeast often acts faster in hotter weather (85°F and up), so you need less yeast. Try reducing the yeast by 1/2 teaspoon. In humid weather, your flour can absorb the moisture in the air. Try reducing the water in your recipe by about 1 tablespoon. With experimentation and patience, you will become an expert on how to mix your ingredients to match your climate.

PADDLE BAKES INTO BREAD

The loaf appears normal, but the paddle comes out of the machine with the bread. Although this is not desirable, it is normal for some bread machines with a detachable paddle. Remove the paddle from the bread, but do not use a hard metal utensil that might scratch the paddle's surface. Try a chopstick.

CHAPTER FOUR

Ensuring Success:

Tips for Bread Machine Bakers

Even though you might feel intimidated at first, take a look at your bread dough several times during the kneading process and while it is rising. This way, you will learn to recognize the proper consistency of the perfect loaf. After you have an idea of how the dough should look, when you try a new recipe, you can check the dough halfway through the mixing cycle and prevent a possible failure. If the dough looks too wet, add approximately 1 tablespoon of flour. If the dough seems too dry, add liquid 1 tablespoon at a time.

MEASURING TIPS

Careful, precise measurements make the difference between a great loaf and a flop.

Use a good quality kitchen scale for the most accurate measurements.

In this recipe book you will find cup measures and weights, listed in ounces, given for the primary flours and liquids used. The reason is that a cup of flour can vary several ounces in weight depending on how roughly the sack of flour was handled and how tightly you pack flour into a cup. So, to be sure, double-check your measurements by spooning the flour (or pouring

27

the water) into the container that is on a good kitchen scale. It might take a few more seconds, but consistently perfect loaves are worth the effort.

Measure dry ingredients in a cup designed for dry ingredients.
You'll get a more accurate measure and a better loaf if you use proper equipment. Dry measuring cups typically come in a set of four metal cups with the following sizes: $1/4$ cup, $1/3$ cup, $1/2$ cup, and 1 cup. Scoop the ingredients into the measuring cup, then tap the cup lightly to settle. Lightly overfill the cup size needed, then use a knife or other flat utensil to even the top for accuracy. The top should be level.

Measure liquids in a cup or beaker designed for measuring liquids.
Use a clear glass or plastic measuring cup or beaker to measure liquids. Always set the measuring cup on a flat surface for the most accurate reading.

Use standard measuring spoons.
When you use teaspoons or tablespoons, use standard measuring spoons. Table flatware is not designed for accurate measuring.

Measurement Equivalents

$1 1/2$ teaspoons	=	$1/2$ tablespoon
3 teaspoons	=	1 tablespoon
4 tablespoons	=	$1/4$ cup
$5 1/3$ tablespoons	=	$1/3$ cup
2 tablespoons	=	$1/8$ cup
16 tablespoons	=	1 cup

KNOW YOUR BREAD MACHINE

Bread machines differ in the size loaf they can make. Basically, if the recipe book accompanying your machine typically calls for 2 cups of flour, you should use the 1-pound recipes in this book. If your machine's recipes usually call for 3 cups of flour, you can use our 1-pound or 1 1/2-pound recipes.

Some machines require wet ingredients to be added first, followed by dry ingredients, with the yeast being added last. Other machines reverse this order. Be sure to add the ingredients in the order requested for your particular machine. You will get the best results from all the recipes if you follow your machine's specifications carefully.

MISCELLANEOUS RECIPE TIPS

Dried fruits, vegetables, spices, and herbs should be put in the bread pan with other dry ingredients. Keep them separate from the liquid so they don't absorb water and throw off the liquid-to-flour ratio. Try adding half the flour, then any dried fruits or vegetables, any spices or herbs, and finally the remaining half of the flour to ensure these ingredients do not absorb water.

Be sure to allow for the additional moisture content in cheese when you add this ingredient to recipes. For example, if you're adding 3 ounces (as measured by weight) of a grated hard cheese such as cheddar, reduce the liquid content of the recipe by about 30 percent of the weight of your cheese, or 1 ounce. In this example, if you were adding 3 ounces of hard cheese and the original recipe called for 1 cup (8 ounces) of water, you would only add 7 ounces of water.

Slightly warm water (80 – 85°F) works best for most recipes. This is the temperature that best supports the yeast's activity. If water is much colder, the yeast is inactive or sluggish. If water is much hotter, the yeast dies.

Tips for Using Your Bread Machine's Timer

When you're using your bread machine's timer, it is even more essential to measure ingredients properly because you won't be there to doctor the dough if it is too dry or wet.

Never use perishable ingredients when using the timer delay. Ingredients such as eggs or dairy products can spoil in as little as 2 hours.

When using your timer, add your ingredients in an order that keeps the yeast away from any liquid or moist ingredients. Liquid activates the yeast.

Storage Tips

Be sure to allow fresh-baked bread to cool at least 20 to 30 minutes before you cut slices and at least an hour before you bag it for storage. If stored in plastic before it has completely cooled, the warm bread will "sweat" inside the bag, and you'll end up with a soggy crust.

Your bread will keep best — from 3 days to a week — in a heavy plastic bag, such as a Ziploc™, outside the refrigerator in a bread box. Storing bread in the refrigerator usually causes the bread to dry out more quickly.

If you wish to store your bread for longer periods of time, freeze it. If possible, freeze loaves whole. Slicing exposes more surface area, which may result in an off flavor. Be sure to wrap your bread well in plastic wrap or place it in a plastic storage bag to prevent freezer burn. To defrost, remove the bread from the freezer, discard the plastic wrap, rewrap the bread in aluminum foil, and place it in a 350°F (177°C) oven for about 20 to 40 minutes, depending on the density of your bread and how solidly frozen the loaf is. Your bread will taste fresh baked.

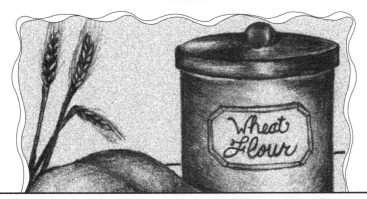

CHAPTER FIVE

Basic Wheat and Grain Breads

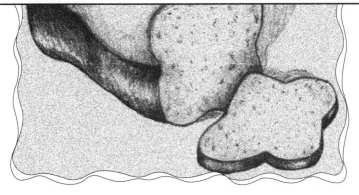

Wheat

Wheat is the oldest and most widely cultivated of the cereal grains. Wheat feeds more people than any other grain and is grown on more land than any other food. In fact, more than 22 percent of all cropland in the world is used for growing wheat. The U.S. grows more wheat than any other nation; and Kansas, North Dakota, Oklahoma, Texas, Washington, and Montana are the leading wheat-producing states.

Whole wheat is rich in nutrients and is a good source of all the B vitamins (except B12), vitamin E, potassium, magnesium, iron, zinc, phosphorous, and selenium. When wheat is refined, however, it loses the bran and germ, which contain the fiber and most of the nutrients. All that remains is the starchy endosperm, which is then bleached and chemically treated. Of the 22 nutrients removed by this refining process, only 3 B vitamins and iron must by law be added back for flour to be labeled enriched. For bread baking, look for whole wheat flour (stone-milled whole wheat flour is best) and store it in your refrigerator or freezer to prevent rancidity. Unless the label says *whole* or *100% whole* in front of the word wheat, the wheat flour is refined. When you purchase such wheat flour, look for an unbleached brand that has fewer chemicals added.

Basic Whole Wheat Bread

A classic loaf that is great for sandwiches or as a hearty accompaniment to any meal. Try adding nuts, dried fruit, or other grains to create your own delicious variations.

1-pound loaf (8 – 10 servings):

1 cup water
1 tablespoon canola oil
2 teaspoons honey
1 teaspoon salt
3 tablespoons wheat germ
2 cups (10.8 ounces) whole wheat flour
1 1/2 tablespoons gluten flour
1 tablespoon powdered whey
1 1/2 teaspoons active dry yeast

1 1/2-pound loaf (12 – 14 servings):

1 1/4 cups water
1 1/2 tablespoons canola oil
1 tablespoon honey
2 teaspoon salt
1/4 cup wheat germ
3 cups (16.2 ounces) whole wheat flour
2 tablespoons gluten flour
1 1/2 tablespoons powdered whey
2 teaspoons active dry yeast

Put the ingredients in the bread pan in the order listed. Reverse the order if the manual for your machine calls for dry ingredients first. Select Basic Wheat Cycle, Light Setting (or the equivalent setting for your machine). Press Start.

Nutrient analysis per Serving
Calories: 114
Carbohydrates: 21
Protein: 4
Fat: 2
Fiber: 4

Bran

Bran is the outer covering of whole grains and is mostly composed of cellulose, an indigestible plant fiber. Bran also contains approximately 19 percent of the grain's protein and 73 percent of its vitamin B6, as well as many other B vitamins and trace amounts of several minerals.

Studies show that oat bran binds cholesterol and removes it from the body, thereby lowering the risk of cardiovascular disease. Too much bran, however, can interfere with the absorption of important nutrients. Wheat bran contains fiber compounds called *phytates*. These compounds bind with and impair the absorption of calcium, zinc, iron, and copper. Excessive bran can cause bloating or constipation. If you are regularly using more than 1/3 cup of wheat bran per day, you might want to supplement your diet with additional minerals. Avoid using more than 1/3 cup of bran in a 1-pound loaf, or 1/2 cup in a 1 1/2 -pound loaf of bread.

Bran Bread

A truly satisfying bread with all the goodness of whole grains plus extra fiber.

1-pound loaf (8–10 servings):

1 cup water
1 tablespoon canola oil
1 tablespoon honey
1 teaspoon salt
1/8 cup oat bran
1/3 cup wheat bran
1 1/2 cups (8.1 ounces) whole wheat flour
2/3 cup (3.4 ounces) unbleached flour
2 tablespoons gluten flour
1 tablespoon powdered whey
1 1/2 teaspoons active dry yeast

1 1/2-pound loaf (12–14 servings):

1 1/2 cups water
1 1/2 tablespoons canola oil
1 1/2 tablespoons honey
2 teaspoons salt
1/4 cup oat bran
1/2 cup wheat bran
2 cups (10.8 ounces) whole wheat flour
1 cup (5.2 ounces) unbleached flour
3 tablespoons gluten flour
1/2 tablespoons powdered whey
2 1/2 teaspoons active dry yeast

Put the ingredients in the bread pan in the order listed. Reverse the order if the manual for your machine calls for dry ingredients first. Select Basic Wheat Cycle, Light Setting (or the equivalent setting for your machine). Press Start.

RECIPE TIP

Bread recipes that contain extra bran may need a little extra water.

Nutrient Analysis per Serving
Calories: 127
Carbohydrates: 23
Protein: 4
Fat: 2
Fiber: 3

35

Fiber

Fiber is an absolutely essential part of a healthy diet. According to National Cancer Institute recommendations, a health-promoting diet should include 25 to 35 grams of dietary fiber each day. This amount can easily be consumed when eating a diet based on whole grains, raw fruits and vegetables, nuts, seeds, and legumes (beans, peas, and lentils). To increase your intake of fiber:

- Make whole grains and other complex carbohydrates the foundation of your healthy diet. This means eating 6 to 11 servings chosen from bread, cereal, rice, and pasta daily. Just 1 slice of whole wheat bread can provide up to 3 grams of fiber.

- Eat 3 to 5 servings of vegetables and 2 to 4 servings of fruit daily.

- Substitute soluble fiber and protein-rich bean dishes and soups for fiberless meat and fish dishes.

Oatmeal Wheat Bread

The addition of oats to this basic wheat bread lends a chewy texture and delicate light oat taste.

1-pound loaf (8 – 10 servings):

3/4 cup water
1 teaspoon salt
2 teaspoons canola oil
2 teaspoons honey
3/4 cup (3.9 ounces) unbleached flour
3/4 cup (4.1 ounces) whole wheat flour
1 tablespoon wheat germ
1/3 cup oats
1 tablespoon powdered whey
1 1/2 teaspoons active dry yeast

1 1/2-pound loaf (12 – 14 servings):

1 cup plus 2 tablespoons water
2 teaspoons salt
1 tablespoon canola oil
1 tablespoon honey
1 cup (5.2 ounces) unbleached flour
1 1/4 cups (6.8 ounces) whole wheat flour
1 1/2 tablespoons wheat germ
1/2 cup oats
1 1/2 tablespoons powdered whey
2 teaspoons active dry yeast

Put the ingredients in the bread pan in the order listed. Reverse the order if the manual for your machine calls for dry ingredients first. Select Basic Wheat Cycle, Light Setting (or the equivalent setting for your machine). Press Start.

Nutrient Analysis per Serving
Calories: 124
Carbohydrates: 23
Protein: 5
Fat: 2

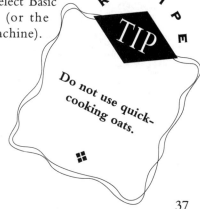

RECIPE TIP

Do not use quick-cooking oats.

Wheat Germ

Wheat germ is the embryo or growth portion of the wheat kernel, the storehouse of the wheat's protein, essential fats, vitamins, and minerals. It is by far the most healthful portion of the entire grain and can be used to enhance the quality and quantity of protein in cookies, muffins, grain-based casseroles, and sometimes even beverages. It also makes a great topping for cereal, pudding, or fruit. Unfortunately, wheat germ is more commonly an ingredient in livestock feed, as it is greatly under-valued by Americans. As a result, our livestock benefit from the full complement of nutrients in wheat germ, but most Americans do not.

Some people prefer the crunchy texture and nutty taste of toasted wheat germ over raw. Toasting only slightly reduces its nutritional value. Presweetened brands, however, contain on average an added teaspoon of refined sugar per cup and should be avoided. Defatted wheat germ is also to be avoided, as it lacks the germ's essential fatty acids, which are important for maintaining human health. Since wheat germ is highly perishable, be certain to purchase it in vacuum-packed containers to assure freshness; store it in the refrigerator to prevent rancidity after opening, and use it up quickly.

100% Wheat Bread

The perfect bread for hearty meals! The addition of unbleached flour gives this loaf a lighter, more consistent crumb than traditional whole wheat bread. You'll love its versatility.

1-pound loaf (8 – 10 servings):
- 1 cup water
- 1 teaspoon salt
- 1 1/2 tablespoons canola oil
- 1 1/4 tablespoons honey
- 1 1/2 cups (8.1 ounces) whole wheat flour
- 2/3 cup (3.5 ounces) unbleached flour
- 2 tablespoons gluten flour
- 1 1/2 tablespoons wheat germ
- 1 1/4 teaspoons powdered whey
- 2 teaspoons active dry yeast

1 1/2-pound loaf (12 – 14 servings):
- 1 1/4 cups water
- 1 1/2 teaspoons salt
- 2 tablespoons canola oil
- 2 tablespoons honey
- 2 cups plus 2 tablespoons (11.5 ounces) whole wheat flour
- 3/4 cup (3.9 ounces) unbleached flour
- 3 tablespoons gluten flour
- 2 tablespoons wheat germ
- 2 tablespoons powdered whey
- 1 tablespoon active dry yeast

Put the ingredients in the bread pan in the order listed. Reverse the order if the manual for your machine calls for dry ingredients first. Select Basic Wheat Cycle, Light Setting (or the equivalent setting for your machine). Press Start.

Nutrient Analysis per Serving:
Calories: 129
Carbohydrates: 23
Protein: 5
Fat: 2
Fiber: 3

Honey

Honey is created by bees from flower nectar and is probably the most popular sweetener for healthful baked products. Raw honey contains small amounts of nutrients and bee pollen, which contains enzymes that aid in digestion. Pure honey has been heated to high temperatures and has had the pollen removed. Although nutrients are lost in the heating process, no chemicals or bleaches are used to produce honey, unlike the refining process for white and brown sugars.

Honey is up to 60 percent sweeter than white sugar, so you need only half as much sweetener when substituting honey for sugar in recipes. If you are substituting honey for another sweetener, reduce the liquid in the recipe by 1/4 cup per cup of honey used.

Because honey can contain spores of botulism, a potentially dangerous bacterium that can accumulate in an infant's immature intestines and form a deadly toxin, honey should never be given to infants. Infant botulism is different from the botulism that can occur from eating improperly canned or cooked foods and does not occur in older children or adults.

Buttermilk Bread

Buttermilk is a cultured or soured milk made from pasteurized skim milk. It adds a spark to any dish, such as this variation on traditional white bread.

1-pound loaf (8 – 10 servings):
  2/3 cup buttermilk
  2 (10.4 ounces) cups unbleached flour
  1 1/4 tablespoons butter or margarine
  2 tablespoons honey
  1 teaspoon salt
  1 1/2 teaspoons active dry yeast

1 1/2-pound loaf (12 – 14 servings):
  1 cup buttermilk
  3 (15.6 ounces) cups unbleached flour
  2 tablespoons butter or margarine
  3 tablespoons honey
  1 1/2 teaspoons salt
  2 teaspoons active dry yeast

Put the ingredients in the bread pan in the order listed. Reverse the order if the manual for your machine calls for dry ingredients first. Select Basic White Cycle. Press Start. Do not use your timer function for this recipe.

Nutrient Analysis per Serving:
Calories: 126
Carbohydrates: 27
Protein: 3
Fat: 2
Fiber: 1

The History of Cereal

In 1895, Dr. John Kellogg, a young doctor recently hired to run the Seventh-Day Adventist's Battle Creek Sanitarium in Michigan, had an accident. Some pans full of bread dough were left sitting while he was called away on an emergency. When he returned, he ran the dough through rollers to turn it into thin sheets to be toasted and ground into flour. Instead of sheets, however, the rollers produced a bunch of flakes. A man tight with a dollar, Kellogg toasted the flakes and served them to his patients. They loved them, and cereal flakes were born. Kellogg and his staff came up with two flake variations — rice and corn. The corn was a flop until someone decided to use only the heart of the corn and flavor it with malt. Instantly, the corn flakes became such a success that Dr. Kellogg set up the Sanitarium Health Food Company with his brother Will, and in its first year, the company sold over 100,000 pounds of flakes.

Sister Ellen White, the devoutly religious founder of Battle Creek Sanitarium, was furious; she felt Dr. Kellogg had turned the sanitarium into a "cereal Sodom." Will Kellogg, however, was pressuring his brother to cash in on their products. While opposed to such practices, Dr. Kellogg found that his business kept growing. He kept getting wealthier, but in lieu of giving pay raises to employees, he gave out stock in the company instead — stock that brother Will quietly bought until 1906, when he gained control of the company. Dr. Kellogg felt so betrayed that he never spoke to his brother again.

White Bread

This is the simple, traditional recipe we all love.

1-pound loaf (8 – 10 servings):
2/3 cup milk
2 cups (10.4 ounces) unbleached flour
1 1/2 tablespoons honey
1 teaspoon salt
1 1/2 tablespoons butter or margarine
1 1/2 teaspoons active dry yeast
(2 1/2 tablespoons powdered milk)

1 1/2-pound loaf (12 – 14 servings):
1 cup milk
3 cups (15.6 ounces) unbleached flour
2 tablespoons honey
1 1/2 teaspoons salt
2 tablespoons butter or margarine
2 teaspoons active dry yeast
(1/4 cup powdered milk)

Put the ingredients in the bread pan in the order listed. Reverse the order if the manual for your machine calls for dry ingredients first. Select Basic White Cycle. Press Start.

If you are going to use your bread machine's timer function in this recipe, you should substitute water for milk. Then add powdered milk to your dry ingredients.

Nutrient Analysis per Serving:
Calories: 134
Carbohydrates: 24
Protein: 4
Fat: 2
Fiber: 1

Almost Fat-Free
Hummus

Here is a quickly made, tasty spread that adds nutritional power to French bread.

    1 15-ounce can cooked garbanzos
    2 to 3 tablespoons water, if needed
    1/4 cup lemon juice, freshly extracted, if possible
    2 to 3 tablespoons maple syrup
    1/2 small sweet onion, chopped
    1 small raw carrot, chopped
    1/8 fresh green pepper, seeded
    1/2 teaspoon ground coriander
    1/4 teaspoon paprika
    dash cayenne
    2 to 3 drops toasted sesame oil
    2 tablespoons fresh minced parsley
    1 to 2 fresh mint leaves or sprigs of parsley for garnish

Drain garbanzos. If you are trying to reduce your intake of sodium, discard the liquid. If not, reserve. In a blender or food processor, puree garbanzos with lemon juice and maple syrup. Add onion, carrot, green pepper, coriander, paprika, cayenne, toasted sesame oil, and parsley. Process until consistency is smooth and creamy, adding reserved liquid from beans or water if necessary. Cover and refrigerate until 1/2 hour before serving. Garnish with mint or parsley.

French Bread

Olive oil gives this french bread a rich, slightly fruity flavor.

Good

1-pound loaf (8 – 10 servings):
$3/4$ cup water
1 $1/2$ teaspoons olive oil
2 (10.4 ounces) cups unbleached flour
$3/4$ teaspoon sugar
$3/4$ teaspoon salt
1 teaspoon active dry yeast

1 $1/2$-pound loaf (12 – 14 servings):
1 $1/8$ cups water
1 tablespoon olive oil
3 (15.6 ounces) cups unbleached flour
1 $1/4$ teaspoons sugar
1 teaspoon salt
2 teaspoons active dry yeast

Put the ingredients in the bread pan in the order listed. Reverse the order if the manual for your machine calls for dry ingredients first. Select French Bread Cycle or Basic White Cycle. Press Start.

Nutrient Analysis per Serving:
Calories: 99
Carbohydrates: 20
Protein: 3
Fat: 1
Fiber: 1

Water

Water is the single most important nutrient for mankind. Humans and animals can survive longer without food than without water. Water is necessary for the life and shape of every cell and accounts for about 75 percent of an infant's body weight and 50 to 65 percent of an adult's. Water plays a critical role in regulating body temperature and is essential for the elimination of wastes by way of the kidneys and intestines. Water also is a source of minerals that are important for cardiovascular health. All foods contain water. Fresh vegetables and juicy fruits contain the most; for example, lettuce is 95 percent water, and watermelon is 93 percent water. For optimal health, drink 64 ounces, or 8 glasses, of water each day in addition to the liquid you consume in freshly extracted vegetable or fruit juices.

Italian Wheat Bread

A hearty wheat bread with a delicious addition—pesto!
Serve with a crisp green salad and your favorite pasta.

1-pound loaf (8–10 servings):
2/3 cup water
1 tablespoon honey
1/2 teaspoon salt
1/4 cup pesto
1 1/2 cups (8.1 ounces) whole wheat flour
1/2 cup (2.6 ounces) unbleached flour
2 1/2 teaspoons gluten flour
1 1/2 teaspoons active dry yeast

1 1/2-pound loaf (12–14 servings):
1 cup water
1 1/2 tablespoons honey
3/4 teaspoon salt
1/3 cup pesto
2 1/4 cups (12.2 ounces) whole wheat flour
3/4 cup (3.9 ounces) unbleached flour
2 tablespoons gluten flour
2 teaspoons active dry yeast

Put the ingredients in the bread pan in the order listed. Reverse the order if the manual for your machine calls for dry ingredients first. Select Basic Wheat Cycle, Light Setting (or the equivalent setting for your machine). Press Start.

Nutrient Analysis per Serving:
Calories: 109
Carbohydrates: 20
Protein: 3
Fat: 2
Fiber: 3

Ginger

Ginger comes from a Sanskrit word meaning "horn-shaped" and is a rhizome, or underground stem, resembling a thickened root. Ginger has been used by the Chinese as far back as the sixth century B.C. By the Middle Ages, ginger was widely used, appearing in practically every sauce recipe. In the sixteenth century, Spain introduced ginger to the West Indies. Today, you can find fresh ginger in most grocery stores, and its strong, unique flavor is a delightful addition to many dishes. However, until you get accustomed to its intense taste, use ginger with caution. When you select ginger, choose a piece that is rock-hard and sturdy. Wrap the ginger in paper toweling or a brown paper bag, then put it in a plastic bag and refrigerate. Change the paper when it becomes moist, usually within a week. If stored in this fashion, ginger will keep for several weeks. If the ginger has been washed well, there's no need to peel it before use.

Oatmeal Ginger Bread

A hearty, chewy whole grain bread with a special touch of spice.

1-pound loaf (8 – 10 servings):

3/4 cup water
1 tablespoon canola oil
2 tablespoons molasses
1 teaspoon salt
1/2 teaspoon ground ginger
1 2/3 cups (9 ounces) whole wheat flour
2/3 cup rolled oats
2 tablespoons gluten flour
1 1/2 tablespoons powdered whey
1 1/2 teaspoons active dry yeast

1 1/2-pound loaf (12 – 14 servings):

1 1/4 cups water
1 1/2 tablespoons canola oil
3 tablespoons molasses
1 1/2 teaspoons salt
1 teaspoon ground ginger
2 1/2 cups (13.5 ounces) whole wheat flour
1 cup rolled oats
3 tablespoons gluten flour
2 tablespoons powdered whey
2 teaspoons active dry yeast

Put the ingredients in the bread pan in the order listed. Reverse the order if the manual for your machine calls for dry ingredients first. Select Basic Wheat Cycle, Light Setting (or the equivalent setting for your machine). Press Start.

Nutrient Analysis per Serving:
Calories: 151
Carbohydrates: 27
Protein: 6
Fat: 3
Fiber: 4

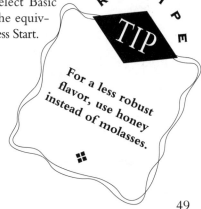

RECIPE TIP

For a less robust flavor, use honey instead of molasses.

Pumpernickel

Pumpernickel is a sourdough bread made from unsifted rye flour. It is usually sold as a blend of white or wheat flour with dark rye flour and sometimes coarse rye meal. Its dark color is often enhanced with molasses, coffee, postum, carob, and sometimes caramel coloring (although this is less desirable). Because homemade pumpernickel bread usually contains more rye than rye breads made from white and rye flours, it also contains more calcium, magnesium, potassium, and lysine than store-bought pumpernickel.

Pumpernickel Bread

Very good

Its rich color and full flavor will make this loaf a favorite of pumpernickel connoisseurs.

1-pound loaf (8 – 10 servings):

3/4 cup plus 2 tablespoons water
2 tablespoons canola oil
1 1/2 tablespoons honey
2 1/2 tablespoons molasses
1 teaspoon salt
1 1/3 cups (7.2 ounces) whole wheat flour
2/3 cup (2.7 ounces) rye flour
3 tablespoons gluten flour
2 tablespoons cornmeal
1/4 teaspoon instant coffee
1 teaspoon caraway seeds
1 tablespoon powdered whey
2 1/2 teaspoons active dry yeast

1 1/2-pound loaf (12 – 14 servings):

1 1/2 cups water
3 tablespoons canola oil
2 tablespoons honey
3 1/2 tablespoons molasses
1 1/2 teaspoons salt
2 cups (10.8 ounces) whole wheat flour
1 cup (4.1 ounces) rye flour
5 tablespoons gluten flour
1/4 cup cornmeal
1/2 teaspoon instant coffee
1 1/2 teaspoons caraway seeds
1 1/2 tablespoons powdered whey
3 1/4 teaspoons active dry yeast

Put the ingredients in the bread pan in the order listed. Reverse the order if the manual for your machine calls for dry ingredients first. Select Basic Wheat Cycle, Light Setting (or the equivalent setting for your machine). Press Start.

Nutrient Analysis per Serving:
Calories: 157
Carbohydrates: 28
Protein: 5
Fat: 4
Fiber: 3

Rye

Rye is a hardy grain capable of flourishing in adverse climates and poor soils. Most people think rye originated in Central Asia before spreading westward into Eastern Europe over 2,000 years ago.

Rye can be cooked whole and is particularly delicious when mixed with other grains. Rye flakes, which can be found at many natural food stores, are delicious toasted and added to a favorite granola recipe. Rye is hardy and has a very strong flavor, attributable to its weedlike heritage. Low in gluten, rye flour works best when used in unleavened baked goods or in combination with wheat flour and a leavening agent. In the mid-1950s, scientists crossbred rye with wheat in hopes of obtaining a grain high in gluten and capable of growing in poorer, drier soils under more severe climate conditions. The attempt was successful and the combination of these two grains is known as triticale.

Light Rye Bread

A lighter version of the traditional rye loaf, this loaf rises higher and is more versatile than dark rye.

1-pound loaf (8 – 10 servings):

- 3/4 cup water
- 1 1/2 tablespoons honey
- 1 tablespoon canola oil
- 3/4 teaspoon salt
- 3/4 cup (4.1 ounces) whole wheat flour
- 3/4 cup (3.9 ounces) unbleached flour
- 1/2 cup (2.1 ounces) rye flour
- 2 tablespoons gluten flour
- 2 teaspoons cornmeal
- 1 teaspoon caraway seeds
- 1 1/2 teaspoons active dry yeast

1 1/2-pound loaf (12 – 14 servings):

- 1 cup plus 2 tablespoons water
- 2 1/4 tablespoons honey
- 1 1/2 tablespoons canola oil
- 1 1/4 teaspoons salt
- 1 1/4 cups (6.8 ounces) whole wheat flour
- 1 cup (5.2 ounces) unbleached flour
- 3/4 cup (3.1 ounces) rye flour
- 3 tablespoons gluten flour
- 1 tablespoon cornmeal
- 1/2 tablespoon caraway seeds
- 2 teaspoons active dry yeast

Put the ingredients in the bread pan in the order listed. Reverse the order if the manual for your machine calls for dry ingredients first. Select Basic Wheat Cycle, Light Setting (or the equivalent setting for your machine). Press Start.

Nutrient Analysis per Serving:
Calories: 124
Carbohydrates: 23
Protein: 4
Fat: 2
Fiber: 2

RECIPE TIP

Expect this bread to be dense and slow-rising, but also expect great flavor!

Cracked Wheat

Also known as bulgur, cracked wheat is made by crushing toasted and briefly boiled wheat berries, which are the original form of whole wheat. Used in cooked cereals, breads, soups, casseroles, and starchy vegetables, bulgur has a nutty taste and texture, is an excellent source of potassium (390 mg per 100 grams), and is very low in sodium (3 mg per 100 grams). It can be eaten as is after a brief soaking or is easily cooked in 15 to 20 minutes. Use only small amounts of bulgur in bread baking because the sharp edges of its fine particles cut the gluten, resulting in a dough that is too elastic.

Multi-Grain Bread

V. good
— especially my
version

No time for hot cereals for breakfast? Try this bread!

1-pound loaf (8 – 10 servings):

3/4 cup water
1 tablespoon oil
1 1/2 tablespoons honey
1 teaspoon salt
1 cup (5.4 ounces) whole wheat flour
1/3 cup (1.7 ounces) unbleached flour
2 tablespoons gluten flour
3 tablespoons multi-grain cereal
2 tablespoons wheat germ
1 tablespoon oat bran
1 1/2 tablespoons cracked wheat
1 1/2 tablespoons powdered whey
1 1/2 teaspoons active dry yeast

1 1/2-pound loaf (12 – 14 servings):

1 1/4 cups water
1 1/2 tablespoons oil
2 tablespoons honey
1 1/2 teaspoons salt
2 cups (10.8 ounces) whole wheat flour
1/2 cup (2.6 ounces) unbleached flour
3 1/2 tablespoons gluten flour
1/3 cup multi-grain cereal
3 tablespoons wheat germ
2 tablespoons oat bran
2 tablespoons cracked wheat
2 tablespoons powdered whey
2 teaspoons active dry yeast

± 1 3/7 *± 1 6/7*

Rolled oats 1/4 C
Flax 1T
millet 1T
Sunflower 1T
Sesame 1T
W. Bran 2T
W. germ 2T
Oat bran 2T
Cracked W 2T

Put the ingredients in the bread pan in the order listed, or in the reverse order if the manual for your machine calls for dry ingredients first and liquids last. Select Basic Wheat Cycle, Light Setting (or the equivalent setting for your machine). Push Start.

Nutrient Analysis per Serving:
Calories: 130
Carbohydrates: 23
Protein: 5
Fat: 2
Fiber: 3

55

Sourdough Starter

Here is an easy method for preparing a sourdough starter, sourdough bread's key ingredient .

2 cups lukewarm milk (110 to 115° F)
2 cups bread flour
1 1/2 teaspoons sugar
2 1/2 teaspoons (one pkg.) active dry yeast

Combine all ingredients in a plastic or glass bowl. Using plastic spoon, mix until smooth. Cover loosely and store at warm room temperature for 5 to 10 days.

Your starter will begin to ferment and bubble. Stir once or twice a day with a plastic spoon. If your starter displays a purple tinge, discard and begin again.

After using part of your starter, feed the remainder with the following mixture. Add to the starter an equal amount of liquid and bread flour for each amount you have used. It is recommended that you switch between using milk and water in feeding your starter. If you have used 1 cup of starter, for example, add 1 cup bread flour and 1 cup water to the remainder. Next time, feed it with milk and bread flour.

After your starter has been used and fed, store at room temperature for 1 day. Then refrigerate, loosely covered. Feed your unused refrigerated starter by adding 1 teaspoon of sugar every 10 days.

Sourdough Bread

The tanginess of sourdough makes this bread a favorite for toast and sandwiches.

1-pound loaf (8 – 10 servings):
3/4 cup sourdough starter (see facing page)

6 tablespoons water

1 tablespoon olive oil

1 dash baking soda

1 1/4 tablespoons sugar

1 1/2 teaspoons salt

2 cups (10.4 ounces) bread flour

1 teaspoon active dry yeast

1 1/2-pound loaf (12 – 14 servings):
1 cup sourdough starter (see facing page)

2/3 cup water

1 1/2 tablespoons olive oil

1/8 teaspoon baking soda

2 tablespoons sugar

2 teaspoons salt

3 cups (15.6 ounces) bread flour

1 1/2 teaspoons active dry yeast

Put the ingredients in the bread pan in the order listed. Reverse the order if the manual for your machine calls for dry ingredients first. Select French Bread Cycle or Basic White Cycle. Press Start.

Nutrient Analysis per Serving:
Calories: 165
Carbohydrates: 30
Protein: 5
Fat: 2
Fiber: 1

Kamut

Kamut is an ancient Egyptian grain enjoying a newfound popularity. It was first grown about 4,000 B.C. in the Fertile Crescent. Now available in most natural food stores, kamut makes an excellent, nutritionally superior substitute for wheat. Though related to modern durum (pasta) wheat, kamut has a rich, buttery flavor and is well tolerated by many who are sensitive to wheat.

Kamut makes a wonderful whole wheat pasta comparable in texture to other whole grain pastas but with a richer flavor than semolina, the most commonly used wheat pasta flour. Since this grain has such a unique flavor and excellent nutritional value, many natural foods manufacturers are developing other kamut products including kamut flour and flakes for hot cereal. In comparison to common wheat, kamut is 40 percent higher in protein, contains as much as 65 percent more amino acids, and is richer in 8 out of 9 minerals.

Ancient Grain Bread

2ry

This unique blend of three ancient grains is sure to please.

1-pound loaf (8 – 10 servings):
- 3/4 cup water
- 1 tablespoon canola oil
- 1 teaspoon honey
- 1/3 teaspoon salt
- 2 tablespoons amaranth grain
- 3 tablespoons kamut flakes
- 1/4 cup quinoa flour
- 1 1/4 cups (6.8 ounces) whole wheat flour
- 2/3 cup (3.5 ounces) unbleached flour
- 1 tablespoon gluten flour
- 1 1/3 tablespoons powdered whey
- 1 1/2 teaspoons active dry yeast

1 1/2-pound loaf (12 – 14 servings):
- 1 1/2 cups water
- 1 1/2 tablespoons canola oil
- 1 1/2 teaspoons honey
- 1/2 teaspoon salt
- 3 tablespoons amaranth grain
- 1/4 cup kamut flakes
- 1/3 cup quinoa flour
- 1 3/4 cups (9.5 ounces) whole wheat flour
- 1 cup (5.2 ounces) unbleached flour
- 2 tablespoons gluten flour
- 2 tablespoons powdered whey
- 2 teaspoons active dry yeast

Put the ingredients in the bread pan in the order listed, or in the reverse order if the manual for your machine calls for dry ingredients first and liquids last. Select Basic Wheat Cycle, Light Setting (or the equivalent setting for your machine). Push Start.

Nutrient Analysis per Serving:
Calories: 121
Carbohydrates: 22
Protein: 5
Fat: 2
Fiber: 2

Quinoa

Referred to as the "lost grain of the Incas," quinoa (pronounced keen-wa) has been farmed in the mountain regions of Peru and Bolivia for 3,000 years. In the Incan empire, only potatoes were more widely cultivated. Quinoa was regarded as a sacred plant, and its annual cultivation was conducted with ceremony. After Pizarro's conquest of the Incas in the 1500s, quinoa production declined until the twentieth century. Today, quinoa is being recultivated in South America and, to a lesser extent, in the United States, where it is grown in the Rocky Mountains of Colorado.

Quinoa is often referred to as a "supergrain" because it supplies nearly twice the protein of most grains yet cooks in just 15 to 20 minutes. Quinoa has a unique flavor, but due to its limited production, it is more expensive than other grains. However, its nutritional benefits and unusual flavor are well worth the extra cost. Quinoa is rich in protein and fiber and boasts more iron, essential fats, calcium, and phosphorus than most grains. Because quinoa is low in gluten, it must be combined with wheat flour for successful leavened breads.

Basic Quinoa Bread

The nutty taste of quinoa, the high-protein supergrain, shines through this unique loaf.

1-pound loaf (8 – 10 servings):

3/4 cup plus 1 tablespoon water
1 tablespoon canola oil
1 teaspoon honey
2/3 teaspoon salt
1/3 cup (1.5 ounces) quinoa flour
1 2/3 cups (9 ounces) whole wheat flour
2 tablespoons gluten flour
1 1/2 tablespoons powdered whey
1 1/2 teaspoons active dry yeast

1 1/2-pound loaf (12 – 14 servings):

1 1/4 cups water
1 1/2 tablespoons canola oil
1 1/2 teaspoons honey
1 teaspoon salt
1/2 cup (2 ounces) quinoa flour
2 1/2 cups (13.5 ounces) whole wheat flour
3 tablespoons gluten flour
2 tablespoons powdered whey
2 teaspoons active dry yeast

Put the ingredients in the bread pan in the order listed, or in the reverse order if the manual for your machine calls for dry ingredients first and liquids last. Select Basic Wheat Cycle, Light Setting (or the equivalent setting for your machine). Push Start.

Nutrient Analysis per Serving:
Calories: 121
Carbohydrates: 21
Protein: 5
Fat: 2
Fiber: 3

Spelt

Spelt is a delicious, easy-to-digest whole grain that tastes similar to wheat but is without wheat's allergenic properties. Many people who are wheat-sensitive find they can easily tolerate spelt, which can be used just like wheat but has a nuttier flavor and lower gluten content. Many pastas are now available in health food stores that contain only spelt flour and water. An added plus is that spelt can be grown without the use of chemical herbicides or pesticides.

Up until a few years ago, spelt was difficult to find, but in 1989, a company called Purity Foods introduced spelt food products into the health food market. Today spelt flour, pastas, and other products are available at many natural food stores across the country.

Barley Spelt Bread

A must for people with wheat allergies, this flavorful bread tastes amazingly similar to whole wheat.

1-pound loaf (8 – 10 servings):

$1/2$ cup water
1 tablespoon canola oil
1 $1/2$ tablespoons honey
1 teaspoon salt
$1/3$ cup cooked barley
2 $1/2$ cups (12 ounces) spelt flour
2 tablespoons powdered whey
1 $1/2$ teaspoons active dry yeast

1 $1/2$-pound loaf (12 – 14 servings):

$3/4$ cup water
1 $1/2$ tablespoons canola oil
2 tablespoons honey
1 $1/2$ teaspoons salt
$1/2$ cup cooked barley
3 $1/2$ cups (16.5 ounces) spelt flour
2 tablespoons powdered whey
2 teaspoons active dry yeast

Put the ingredients in the bread pan in the order listed, or in the reverse order if the manual for your machine calls for dry ingredients first and liquids last. Select Basic Wheat Cycle, Light Setting (or the equivalent setting for your machine). Push Start.

Nutrient Analysis per Serving:
Calories: 136
Carbohydrates: 26
Protein: 4
Fat: 2
Fiber: 4

RECIPE TIP

Due to the nature of spelt flour, the top of your loaf may be flat or slightly indented.

Granola

When oats are combined with other grains, nuts, seeds, unsaturated oils, and a small amount of sweetener, the resulting granola cereal can be a healthful and satisfying snack. For a long time campers and natural foods enthusiasts have regarded granola as an ideal, convenient, natural source of long-term energy. However, be sure to read labels when selecting granola. Most store-bought brands contain not only many high-fat ingredients, such as coconut oil, but also excessive amounts of sweeteners, such as honey, brown sugar, white table sugar (sucrose), corn syrup, or dextrose. These additions turn a naturally healthful snack into a veritable junk food. For bread baking, stick to granolas that have very little added fat and sugar.

Branola Bread

Slightly sweet and delightfully chewy, this bread will be a favorite of children of all ages.

1-pound loaf (8 – 10 servings):
3/4 cup plus 1 tablespoon water
1 tablespoon canola oil
1 tablespoon honey
1 teaspoon salt
2/3 cup (3.6 ounces) whole wheat flour
1 cup (5.2 ounces) unbleached flour
1/3 cup oat bran
1/3 cup fat-free granola
1 1/2 tablespoons powdered whey
2 teaspoons active dry yeast

1 1/2-pound loaf (12 – 14 servings):
1 1/4 cups water
1 1/2 tablespoons canola oil
1 1/2 tablespoons honey
1 1/2 teaspoons salt
1 cup (5.4 ounces) whole wheat flour
1 1/2 cups (7.8 ounces) unbleached flour
1/2 cup oat bran
1/2 cup fat-free granola
2 tablespoons powdered whey
2 1/2 teaspoons active dry yeast

Put the ingredients in the bread pan in the order listed, or in the reverse order if the manual for your machine calls for dry ingredients first and liquids last. Select Basic Wheat Cycle, Light Setting (or the equivalent setting for your machine). Push Start.

Nutrient Analysis per Serving:
Calories: 119
Carbohydrates: 21
Protein: 4
Fat: 2
Fiber: 2

R E C I P E

TIP

The addition of granola makes this a dense loaf that may not rise as much as lighter loaves.

Rice

Rice is the most widely consumed staple food in the world. In Eastern Asia, where 94 percent of the world's rice crop is grown, the annual rice consumption per person is an incredible 200 to 400 pounds. In comparison, the U.S. produces just a little more than 1 percent of the total rice crop, and our yearly per person consumption is less than 8 pounds.

Contrary to most people's perception, rice does not have to grow in water. The rice fields, or paddies, are flooded primarily because this is the most efficient method of weed and insect control.

In its unrefined, natural state, rice is an excellent nutritional value. In fact, rice is the most nutritious of all the major cereals. Brown rice has approximately the same caloric content, vitamins, and minerals as whole wheat; fewer, but higher quality proteins; and more carbohydrates and essential fats. For optimal nutrition, brown rice is always the best choice. One cup of brown rice contains only 230 calories, with less than 2 grams of fat.

Rice Bread

Surprisingly rich and moist! Bet you can't keep this bread around for long.

1-pound loaf (8 – 10 servings):
2/3 cup water
1 tablespoon canola oil
1 tablespoon honey
1/2 cup rice, cooked
1 teaspoon salt
1 2/3 cups (9 ounces) whole wheat flour
2 tablespoons gluten flour
1 tablespoon powdered whey
1 1/2 teaspoons active dry yeast

1 1/2-pound loaf (12 – 14 servings):
1 cup plus 1 tablespoon water
1 1/2 tablespoons canola oil
1 1/3 tablespoons honey
2/3 cup rice, cooked
1 1/4 teaspoons salt
2 1/2 cups (13.5 ounces) whole wheat flour
3 tablespoons gluten flour
2 tablespoons powdered whey
2 teaspoons active dry yeast

Put the ingredients in the bread pan in the order listed, or in the reverse order if the manual for your machine calls for dry ingredients first and liquids last. Select Basic Wheat Cycle, Light Setting (or the equivalent setting for your machine). Push Start.

Nutrient Analysis per Serving:
Calories: 101
Carbohydrates: 19
Protein: 2
Fat: 1
Fiber: 3

Millet

Millet is a small, round grain that provides a major part of the diet for many people living in India, Africa, China, and Russia. At one time, millet was an important crop in Europe as well, but when corn and potatoes were introduced, millet diminished in popularity. In Asia and Africa, millet is grown as a seed crop for food, but in Europe and the U.S., it is grown primarily to feed to livestock. In this country, millet is often more commonly thought of as birdseed than a food grain.

Millet requires little refinement beyond the removal of its outer hull and is, therefore, a better source of nutrients than refined grains such as white rice. It is also a good source of protein, superior to that of wheat, corn, or rice. Millet contains no gluten, so by itself its flour is not suitable for breadmaking. In bread and baked goods, millet is added in its whole form to make multi-grain breads. As a staple grain, millet cooks quicker than rice, taking only 15 to 20 minutes on the stove. When cooked longer (30 to 40 minutes) with juice, millet makes a delicious hot porridge. Millet can also be popped, roasted, sprouted, or malted.

Millet Crunch Bread

Here's another whole grain bread with the pleasing texture of millet!

1-pound loaf (8 – 10 servings):

$3/4$ cup water
2 teaspoons canola oil
1 $1/2$ tablespoons honey
$3/4$ teaspoon salt
3 tablespoons millet
$1/3$ cup millet flour
1 cup (5.4 ounces) whole wheat flour
$2/3$ cup (3.5 ounces) unbleached flour)
1 $1/2$ tablespoons gluten flour
1 $1/2$ tablespoons powdered whey
1 $1/2$ teaspoons active dry yeast

1 $1/2$-pound loaf (12 – 14 servings):

1 $1/8$ cups water
1 tablespoon canola oil
2 tablespoons honey
1 teaspoon salt
$1/4$ cup millet
$1/2$ cup millet flour
1 $1/2$ cups (8.1 ounces) whole wheat flour
1 cup (5.2 ounces) unbleached flour
2 tablespoons gluten flour
2 tablespoons powdered whey
2 teaspoons active dry yeast

Put the ingredients in the bread pan in the order listed, or in the reverse order if the manual for your machine calls for dry ingredients first and liquids last. Select Basic Wheat Cycle, Light Setting (or the equivalent setting for your machine). Push Start.

Nutrient Analysis per Serving:
Calories: 135
Carbohydrates: 27
Protein: 5
Fat: 2
Fiber: 3

Whole Grains

Whole grains are great diet foods: they are low in calories but high in fiber and complex carbohydrates. Whole grains are quite satisfying due to their stabilizing effect on blood sugar levels and their great bulk, reducing the urge to binge eat. Whole grains can be added to bread or used as breakfast cereals, side dishes, casseroles, or part of a entrée.

Old-Fashioned Wheat Bread

Down home farm fresh flavor — perfect every time!

1 pound loaf (8–10 servings):

3/4 cup plus 1 tablespoon water
2 teaspoons canola oil
1 1/2 tablespoons honey
1 teaspoon salt
1 2/3 cups (3.5 ounces) unbleached flour
1/3 cup wheat bran
3 tablespoons wheat germ
1/3 cup cracked wheat
1 1/2 tablespoons powdered whey
1 1/2 teaspoons active dry yeast

1 1/2-pound loaf (12–14 servings):

1 1/4 cups water
1 tablespoon canola oil
2 tablespoons honey
1 1/2 teaspoons salt
2 1/2 cups (11.4 ounces) unbleached flour
1/2 cup wheat bran
1/4 cup wheat germ
1/2 cup cracked wheat
2 tablespoons powdered whey
2 teaspoons active dry yeast

Put the ingredients in the bread pan in the order listed, or in the reverse order if the manual for your machine calls for dry ingredients first and liquids last. Select Basic Wheat Cycle, Light Setting (or the equivalent setting for your machine). Push Start.

Nutrient Analysis per Serving:
Calories: 127
Carbohydrates: 25
Protein: 4
Fat: 2
Fiber: 2

Tofu

Tofu, or bean curd as it is sometimes called, is high in protein and relatively low in calories. Once restricted to Oriental and natural food stores, tofu can now be found in nearly every American supermarket, usually in the produce department.

Tofu has a soft, creamy texture and a mild flavor that easily adapts to the flavor of marinades and spices you use. Tofu is often used in place of meat in seasoned dishes such as pasta sauces, casseroles, stews, or soups. And its mild flavor and adaptive qualities make it the ideal substitute in many recipes for soft cheeses and sour cream. Tofu can also be used to produce rich, moist desserts such as cakes, pies, or cheesecakes.

It's necessary to refrigerate tofu because it is highly perishable. Fresh tofu has no odor and a smooth surface. It is packaged in a water bath that you should change daily after you open the package. If tofu develops an undesirable smell or becomes slippery, discard it. Tofu's newfound popularity has resulted in numerous ready-made products, ranging from tofu burgers, hot dogs, and bologna to spreads and dips.

Soy Flour Bread

Tofu, the "meat" of the Orient, gives this bread a deliciously moist texture and rich flavor.

1-pound loaf (8 – 10 servings):
$1/2$ cup water
1 $1/2$ teaspoons canola oil
1 tablespoon honey
$3/4$ cup firm tofu
$3/4$ teaspoon salt
$1/3$ cup soy flour
$2/3$ cup (3.6 ounces) whole wheat flour
$2/3$ cup (3.5 ounces) unbleached flour
1 tablespoon powdered whey
1 $1/2$ teaspoons active dry yeast

1 $1/2$-pound loaf (12 – 14 servings):
$3/4$ cup water
2 teaspoons canola oil
1 $1/2$ tablespoons honey
1 cup firm tofu
1 teaspoon salt
$1/2$ cup soy flour
1 $1/2$ cups (8.1 ounces) whole wheat flour
1 cup (5.2 ounces) unbleached flour
2 tablespoons powdered whey
2 teaspoons active dry yeast

Put the ingredients in the bread pan in the order listed, or in the reverse order if the manual for your machine calls for dry ingredients first and liquids last. Select Basic Wheat Cycle, Light Setting (or the equivalent setting for your machine). Push Start.

Nutrient Analysis per Serving:
Calories: 120
Carbohydrates: 19.5
Protein: 5.9
Fat: 3.3
Fiber: 2.2

Oat Choices

Oat Groats

Unlike most grains, only the inedible hull of oats is removed in the milling process. The bran and the germ remain in the edible portion, known as the groat, making oats a good source of protein, fiber, and many nutrients.

Steel-Cut Oats

This is the least milled type of oat and is produced by slicing the oats. Though they take longer to cook, from 30 to 45 minutes, they're worth the effort — you get a smooth, creamy porridge with unequaled flavor. To speed up cooking time, soak the oats in water or juice overnight in your refrigerator. For extra flavor, try adding some raisins or other dried fruit. By morning the oats will have softened enough to cook in less than half the time.

Rolled or Old-Fashioned Oats

Rolled oats are steel-cut oats taken 2 steps further. First these sliced oats are steamed to soften the starch, then rolled into flakes and dried. These are the most popular and widely available form of oats. Due to the vastly increased surface area, old-fashioned oats cook in a mere 5 minutes.

Triple Oat Bread

A wonderfully hearty bread with all the benefits of oat bran!

1-pound loaf (8 – 10 servings):

3/4 cup plus 1 tablespoon water
2 teaspoons canola oil
2 teaspoons honey
2 tablespoons molasses
1 teaspoon salt
1/2 cup (2.7 ounces) whole wheat flour
1/3 cup (1.7 ounces) unbleached white flour
2 tablespoons gluten flour
2/3 cup rolled oats
1/3 cup oat flour
1/3 cup oat bran
2 tablespoons powdered whey
1 1/2 teaspoons active dry yeast

1 1/2-pound loaf (12 – 14 servings):

1 1/4 cups water
1 tablespoon canola oil
1 tablespoon honey
3 tablespoons molasses
1 1/4 teaspoons salt
3/4 cup (4.1 ounces) whole wheat flour
1/2 cup (2.6 ounces) unbleached white flour
3 tablespoons gluten flour
1 cup rolled oats
1/2 cup oat flour
1/2 cup oat bran
3 tablespoons powdered whey
2 teaspoons active dry yeast

Put the ingredients in the bread pan in the order listed, or in the reverse order if the manual for your machine calls for dry ingredients first and liquids last. Select Basic Wheat Cycle, Light Setting (or the equivalent setting for your machine). Push Start.

Nutrient Analysis per Serving:
Calories: 136
Carbohydrates: 26
Protein: 4
Fat: 2
Fiber: 4

Bean Spreads

Because beans typically contain high amounts of the essential amino acids in which grains are low, and grains contain amino acids missing in beans, bean spreads offer a perfect way to increase the protein quality of whole grain breads. In addition, beans — with the exception of soy, which contains about 50% fat—are very low in fat and high in soluble fiber, so bean spreads are an excellent choice for anyone concerned about the health of their heart and arteries.

Protein Bread

Perfect for your kids — just add fruit spread and drop it in their lunchbox.

1-pound loaf (8 – 10 servings):

1 cup water
1 tablespoon canola oil
1 teaspoon honey
1/3 teaspoon salt
2 tablespoons amaranth grain
3 tablespoons kamut flakes
1/4 cup quinoa flour
1 1/3 cups (7.2 ounces) whole wheat flour
2/3 cup (3.5 ounces) unbleached flour
1 tablespoon gluten flour
1 1/3 tablespoons powdered whey
1 1/2 teaspoons active dry yeast

1 1/2-pound loaf (12 – 14 servings):

1 1/2 cups water
1 1/2 tablespoons canola oil
1 1/2 teaspoons honey
1/2 teaspoon salt
3 tablespoons amaranth grain
1/4 cup kamut flakes
1/3 cup quinoa flour
2 cups (10.8 ounces) whole wheat flour
1 cup (5.2 ounces) unbleached flour
2 tablespoons gluten flour
2 tablespoons powdered whey
2 1/2 teaspoons active dry yeast

Put the ingredients in the bread pan in the order listed, or in the reverse order if the manual for your machine calls for dry ingredients first and liquids last. Select Basic Wheat Cycle, Light Setting (or the equivalent setting for your machine). Push Start.

Nutrient Analysis per Serving:
Calories: 161
Carbohydrates: 25
Protein: 7
Fat: 5
Fiber: 4

Amaranth

No one knows how long amaranth has been cultivated, although evidence exists that it has been grown for as long as 8,000 years in Central and South America. For several hundred years, amaranth has also been cultivated in the high-altitude terrain of the Himalayas; the hill regions of India, Nepal, Pakistan, and China; and the Tibetan plateau.

If Cortez and the Spaniards, who discovered Mexico in the sixteenth century, had been as concerned with cooking as they were with conquest, they would have returned to the Old World with this golden grain, not just Montezuma's gold. The Aztecs felt amaranth made them strong (and they were probably right, because amaranth has a higher protein profile than most grains). Sadly, as well as stealing the Aztecs' gold, Cortez burned all their amaranth fields and forbade them to eat it as part of his campaign to subdue their culture.

Until the middle of this century, amaranth production was limited to just a few small regions in Mexico and Central and South America. Since 1967, however, amaranth has been vigorously promoted by the United States Food and Agriculture Organization. Amaranth is now cultivated in North America, and worldwide production is on the rise.

Amaranth Flake Oat Bread

The unique flavor of amaranth comes through in this versatile sandwich bread.

1-pound loaf (8–10 servings):

3/4 cup plus 1 tablespoon water
1 tablespoon canola oil
1 tablespoon fructose
2/3 teaspoon salt
3/4 cup (4.1 ounces) whole wheat flour
1/2 cup (2.6 ounces) unbleached flour
2 tablespoons gluten flour
1/2 cup amaranth flakes
1/3 cup oat flour
1/3 cup rolled oats
1 tablespoon powdered whey
1 1/2 teaspoons active dry yeast

1 1/2-pound loaf (12–14 servings):

1 1/4 cups water
1 1/2 tablespoons canola oil
1 1/2 tablespoons fructose
1 teaspoon salt
1 1/4 cups (6.8 ounces) whole wheat flour
3/4 cup (3.9 ounces) unbleached flour
3 tablespoons gluten flour
3/4 cup amaranth flakes
1/2 cup oat flour
1/2 cup rolled oats
1 1/2 tablespoons powdered whey
2 teaspoons active dry yeast

Put the ingredients in the bread pan in the order listed, or in the reverse order if the manual for your machine calls for dry ingredients first and liquids last. Select Basic Wheat Cycle, Light Setting (or the equivalent setting for your machine). Push Start.

RECIPE TIP

Wheat, oat, or corn flakes can be substituted for amaranth flakes.

Nutrient Analysis per Serving:
Calories: 127
Carbohydrates: 25
Protein: 5

Fat: 2
Fiber: 2

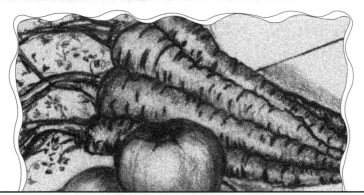

CHAPTER SIX

Vegetable Breads

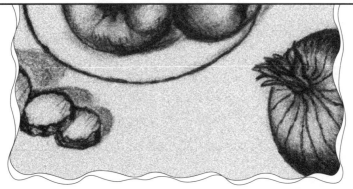

Whey and Whey Protein

Whey is the water and milk solids that remain after the curd in milk is removed. Whey contains about 93 percent water and 7 percent lactose (milk sugar), protein, minerals, enzymes, water-soluble vitamins, and trace amounts of fat. Available in most natural food stores in dried and condensed forms, whey is an inexpensive, easily digested, and nutritious source of lactose, milk solids, and milk proteins. It is used in infant formulas, protein powder drink mixes, and baked goods. Another popular use for whey is as a thickening agent in dessert toppings, soups, and sauces. In breads, whey powder helps ensure a loaf that remains moist but firm.

Zucchini Whole Wheat Bread

Zucchini adds a moist and delicate texture to this hearty whole wheat bread.

1-pound loaf (8 – 10 servings):
3/4 cup water
2 1/2 teaspoons canola oil
1 1/2 tablespoons honey
1/2 cup zucchini, grated
1/2 teaspoon salt
2 cups (10.8 ounces) whole wheat flour
2 tablespoons gluten flour
1 tablespoon powdered whey
1 1/2 teaspoons active dry yeast

1 1/2-pound loaf (12 – 14 servings):
1 cup plus 2 tablespoons water
1 tablespoon canola oil
2 tablespoons honey
3/4 cup zucchini, grated
3/4 teaspoon salt
3 cups (16.2 ounces) whole wheat flour
3 tablespoons gluten flour
1 1/2 tablespoons powdered whey
2 teaspoons active dry yeast

Put the ingredients in the bread pan in the order listed, or in the reverse order if the manual for your machine calls for dry ingredients first and liquids last. Select Basic Wheat Cycle, Light Setting (or the equivalent setting for your machine). Push Start.

Nutrient Analysis per Serving:
Calories: 106
Carbohydrates: 23
Protein: 5
Fat: 1
Fiber: 3

Beans

Garbanzo beans, also called chickpeas, are round, beige beans with a distinct nutty flavor. Aside from their position as a mainstay in bean soups and casserole dishes, garbanzo beans are the main ingredient in the popular Mideastern party dip, hummus. Any kind of bean is an excellent source of dietary fiber, iron, and protein, especially when eaten with grains.

Garbanzo Bread

As delicious at the dinner table as it is in the lunchbox.

1-pound loaf (8 – 10 servings):

3/4 cup plus 1 tablespoon water
2/3 tablespoon canola oil
2 teaspoons Sucanat™
2 teaspoons lemon juice
2/3 cup cooked garbanzo beans
1 teaspoon salt
2 cups (10.8 ounces) whole wheat flour
1 1/2 tablespoons gluten flour
1 1/2 tablespoons powdered whey
1 1/2 teaspoons active dry yeast

1 1/2-pound loaf (12 – 14 servings):

1 1/4 cups water
1 tablespoon canola oil
1 tablespoon Sucanat™
1 tablespoon lemon juice
1 cup cooked garbanzo beans
1 1/4 teaspoons salt
3 cups (16.2 ounces) whole wheat flour
2 tablespoons gluten flour
2 tablespoons powdered whey
2 teaspoon active dry yeast

Put the ingredients in the bread pan in the order listed, or in the reverse order if the manual for your machine calls for dry ingredients first and liquids last. Select Basic Wheat Cycle, Light Setting (or the equivalent setting for your machine). Push Start.

Nutrient Analysis per Serving:
Calories: 109
Carbohydrates: 20
Protein: 5
Fat: 2
Fiber: 4

Carrots

It is thought that carrots originated in the Near East and Central Asia, where they have been grown for thousands of years. The ancient strain of carrot was a purplish color ranging from lavender to nearly black. Carrots were probably first consumed by the Europeans during the Middle Ages, and the vegetable became a staple of their diet in the thirteenth century. In the seventeenth century, European agriculturalists worked on developing the yellow-orange types of carrots and discontinued production of the purple variety.

Carrots are the richest vegetable source of beta-carotene, which the body converts to vitamin A. Vitamin A has been called the anti-infective vitamin and has a direct effect on the health of the immune system.

A mere 2 carrots a day provide roughly 4 times the RDA for vitamin A. Sometimes people who eat or drink large amounts of carrots become alarmed when they notice their skin taking on a yellow-orangish cast. This is not harmful; it merely indicates the storage of excess carotenoids in the skin. The skin color quickly returns to normal when the intake of carotenes is decreased.

Carrot Bread

This mildly flavored, moist bread is a delicious way to get your beta-carotene.

1-pound loaf (8 – 10 servings):

1/3 cup carrot juice
1/2 cup water
2/3 tablespoon canola oil
1 tablespoon molasses
1 tablespoon honey
1 teaspoon salt
1/2 cup grated carrots or carrot pulp from juicing
3/4 cup (4.1 ounces) whole wheat flour
2/3 cup (3.5 ounces) unbleached flour
1 1/2 tablespoons gluten flour
2 teaspoons powdered whey
1 1/2 teaspoons active dry yeast

1 1/2-pound loaf (12 – 14 servings):

1/2 cup carrot juice
1/2 cup water
1 tablespoon canola oil
1 1/2 tablespoons molasses
1 1/2 tablespoons honey
1 1/2 teaspoons salt
3/4 cup grated carrots or carrot pulp from juicing
1 1/3 cups (7.2 ounces) whole wheat flour
1 cup (5.2 ounces) unbleached flour
2 tablespoons gluten flour
1 tablespoon powdered whey
2 teaspoons active dry yeast

Put the ingredients in the bread pan in the order listed, or in the reverse order if the manual for your machine calls for dry ingredients first and liquids last. Select Basic Wheat Cycle, Light Setting (or the equivalent setting for your machine). Push Start.

Nutrient Analysis per Serving:
Calories: 134
Carbohydrates: 26
Protein: 5
Fat: 1
Fiber: 3

Potatoes

Potatoes are widely grown throughout the world and rank behind only the major grains (wheat, rice, and corn) in importance as a staple food. In the United States, the 4 top producing states are Idaho, Washington, Maine, and Oregon.

Contrary to popular belief, potatoes are an ideal diet food, boasting significant nutritive value with few calories. One medium raw potato contains a mere 115 calories, is low in sodium, has more potassium than a medium banana, and a vitamin C content equivalent to about $1/2$ of a medium orange. Unfortunately, most Americans eat the potato in the fat-laden form of french fries, hash browns, or deep-fried potato chips or as baked potatoes smothered with butter and sour cream. That's too bad, because a large baked or microwaved potato is delicious and nutritious and is the perfect carrier for innumerable lowfat toppings. Next time, try topping your baked potato with spaghetti sauce, salsa, cooked beans, bean dip, steamed vegetables, ketchup, or barbecue sauce.

Potato Bread

If you like potatoes, you're certain to love this bread.

2/3 cup potato water
1 tablespoon canola oil
1 tablespoon honey
1/2 cup mashed potatoes
1 teaspoon salt
1 1/3 cups (7.2 ounces) whole wheat flour
2/3 cup (3.5 ounces) unbleached flour
1 1/2 teaspoons active dry yeast

1 1/2-pound loaf (12 – 14 servings):

1 cup potato water
1 1/2 tablespoons canola oil
1 1/3 tablespoons honey
3/4 cup mashed potatoes
1 1/4 teaspoons salt
2 cups (10.8 ounces) whole wheat flour
1 cup (5.2 ounces) unbleached flour
2 teaspoons active dry yeast

Put the ingredients in the bread pan in the order listed, or in the reverse order if the manual for your machine calls for dry ingredients first and liquids last. Select Basic Wheat Cycle, Light Setting (or the equivalent setting for your machine). Push Start.

Nutrient Analysis per Serving:
Calories: 119
Carbohydrates: 22
Protein: 4
Fat: 2
Fiber: 3

RECIPE TIP

Add grated cheese (1/4 cup to the 1-pound loaf or 1/3 cup to 1 1/2-pound loaf) for a potato cheese bread. Add chopped onions (1/3 cup to the 1-pound loaf or 1/4 cup to the 1 1/2-pound loaf) for extra flavor.

Onions

Onions are among the more health-promoting vegetables. Studies show that onions can decrease blood fat levels, help prevent clot formation, and lower blood pressure. Onions also help lower blood sugar, much like prescription drugs often prescribed for diabetics.

The most popular onions — Spanish onions (yellow or white) and Bermuda onions (purplish red) — are the common globe types used for cooking and seasoning. Bermudas are sweeter and make a nice addition in salads. Small white boiling onions and long green onions are referred to as scallions. The Vidalia onion from Georgia, available May through June, and the Walla Walla sweet onion from Washington, harvested in late June through August, are perhaps the most famous onions. Both are favored for their sweet, mild taste.

When choosing onions, look for those with a hard, firm surface and dry skin. Avoid wet, spotted, or soft onions, and be sure to store them in a cool, dry environment.

Onion Poppy Seed Bread

Poppy seeds and onions complement each other in this light and savory bread.

1-pound loaf (8 – 10 servings):

$2/3$ cup water
2 teaspoons canola oil
1 teaspoon honey
$1/4$ cup onions, minced
1 teaspoon salt
2 teaspoons poppy seeds
1 cup (5.4 ounces) whole wheat flour
1 cup (5.2 ounces) unbleached flour
2 teaspoons powdered whey
1 $1/2$ teaspoons active dry yeast

1 $1/2$-pound loaf (12 – 14 servings):

1 cup plus 3 tablespoons water
1 tablespoon canola oil
1 teaspoon honey
$1/3$ cup onions, minced
1 teaspoon salt
1 tablespoon poppy seeds
1 $1/2$ cups (8.1 ounces) whole wheat flour
1 $1/2$ cups (7.8 ounces) unbleached flour
1 tablespoon powdered whey
2 teaspoons active dry yeast

Put the ingredients in the bread pan in the order listed, or in the reverse order if the manual for your machine calls for dry ingredients first and liquids last. Select Basic Wheat Cycle, Light Setting (or the equivalent setting for your machine). Push Start.

Nutrient Analysis per Serving:
Calories: 119
Carbohydrates: 23
Protein: 4
Fat: 2
Fiber: 2

Gluten

Gluten is a plant protein found primarily in wheat. Rye is second to wheat in gluten content, followed by oats and barley, then rice and corn, which have negligible amounts. Gluten is actually made from 2 proteins, gliadin and glutenin, which are mixed together. In bread baking, gluten strands trap the carbon dioxide released by yeast in the process of fermentation, enabling bread to rise properly and maintain its light and lofty height. Some individuals are gluten-sensitive and must eliminate it from their diets. For these individuals, products with flours made from gluten-free grains such as amaranth or rice can be used.

Onion Bread

A spicy twist on an old favorite.

1-pound loaf (8 – 10 servings):

$3/4$ cup water
1 tablespoon canola oil
1 $1/2$ tablespoons honey
1 teaspoon salt
2 cups (10.8 ounces) whole wheat flour
2 tablespoons gluten flour
$1/4$ cup dried onions
$1/2$ teaspoon black pepper
1 $1/2$ tablespoons powdered whey
2 teaspoons active dry yeast

1 $1/2$-pound loaf (12 – 14 servings):

1 $1/2$ cups water
1 $1/2$ tablespoons canola oil
2 tablespoons honey
1 $1/2$ teaspoons salt
3 $1/4$ cups (17.6 ounces) whole wheat flour
4 tablespoons gluten flour
$1/2$ cup dried onions
$3/4$ teaspoon black pepper
2 tablespoons powdered whey
3 teaspoons active dry yeast

Put the ingredients in the bread pan in the order listed, or in the reverse order if the manual for your machine calls for dry ingredients first and liquids last. Select Basic Wheat Cycle, Light Setting (or the equivalent setting for your machine). Push Start.

Nutrient Analysis per Serving:
Calories: 130
Carbohydrates: 24
Protein: 5
Fat: 2
Fiber: 4

Peppers

Select fresh sweet or hot peppers that are firm and brightly colored. Avoid selecting peppers that are shriveled or limp. Hot varieties are available in either the green or red stage and come in all sizes, from the small chile peppers to the large, common bell type. Chile and cayenne peppers are often threaded on strings and dried before they're sold.

Bell Pepper Bread

good - unique
pepper flavor

Moist and spicy — a gardener's delight.

1-pound loaf (8 – 10 servings):
3/4 cup water
1 tablespoon canola oil
1/2 teaspoon honey
1/2 cup bell peppers, diced
1/2 teaspoon salt
1/2 teaspoon dried red pepper flakes
1 1/3 cups (7.2 ounces) whole wheat flour
2/3 cup (3.5 ounces) unbleached flour
1 tablespoon gluten flour
1/4 teaspoon white pepper
1 tablespoon powdered whey
1 1/2 teaspoons active dry yeast

1 1/2-pound loaf (12 – 14 servings):
1 cup plus 3 tablespoons water
1 1/2 tablespoons canola oil
2/3 teaspoon honey
3/4 cup bell peppers, diced
2/3 teaspoon salt
2/3 teaspoon dried red pepper flakes
2 cups (10.8 ounces) whole wheat flour
1 cup (5.2 ounces) unbleached flour
1 1/2 tablespoons gluten flour
1/3 teaspoon white pepper
1 1/2 tablespoons powdered whey
2 teaspoons active dry yeast

Put the ingredients in the bread pan in the order listed, or in the reverse order if the manual for your machine calls for dry ingredients first and liquids last. Select Basic Wheat Cycle, Light Setting (or the equivalent setting for your machine). Push Start.

Nutrient Analysis per Serving:
Calories: 111
Carbohydrates: 20
Protein: 3
Fat: 2
Fiber: 3

Lentils

Lentils are one of the oldest cultivated plants in the world. Archeologists have found lentil seeds at the sites of Middle and Near Eastern farming villages that existed over 8,000 years ago. In addition to providing excellent nutrition, lentils are of particular benefit in managing blood sugar disorders because they reduce the rise in blood glucose levels after a meal.

Lentils, which belong to the legume family of vegetables (dried beans, peanuts), are a good source of iron and an excellent source of complementary proteins when mixed with rice, wheat, or other cereal grains. In contrast to other legumes, lentils require no presoaking and cook quickly (20 – 40) minutes. Lentils are sold as whole dried seeds, as split dried seeds, in flour form, and as an ingredient in canned soups. A staple food in India and the Middle East, lentils can be prepared in a variety of ways but are most commonly combined with vegetables and grains in casseroles, soups, and stews.

Lentil Bread

A classic, hearty winter treat. The combination of lentils and wheat make this bread an excellent source of complete protein.

1-pound loaf (8 – 10 servings):
$3/4$ cup plus 1 tablespoon water
1 tablespoon olive oil
1 tablespoon honey
$1/3$ cup cooked lentils
1 teaspoon salt
1 $1/3$ cups (7.2 ounces) whole wheat flour
$1/3$ cup (1.7 ounces) unbleached flour
1 $1/2$ tablespoons gluten flour
2 tablespoons powdered whey
1 $1/2$ teaspoons active dry yeast

1 $1/2$-pound loaf (12 – 14 servings):
1 $1/4$ cups water
1 $1/2$ tablespoons olive oil
1 $1/2$ tablespoons honey
$3/4$ cup cooked lentils
1 $1/2$ teaspoons salt
2 cups (10.8 ounces) whole wheat flour
1 cup (5.2 ounces) unbleached flour
2 tablespoons gluten flour
3 tablespoons powdered whey
2 teaspoons active dry yeast

Put the ingredients in the bread pan in the order listed, or in the reverse order if the manual for your machine calls for dry ingredients first and liquids last. Select Basic Wheat Cycle, Light Setting (or the equivalent setting for your machine). Push Start.

Nutrient Analysis per Serving:
Calories: 112
Carbohydrates: 2
Protein: 4
Fat: 2
Fiber: 2

Molasses

Molasses is the liquid that remains when white sugar is extracted from sugar cane. It is available in different grades and can contain some minerals from the sugar cane, depending on the extraction and refining process used. Blackstrap molasses is the darkest, most flavorful, and richest in nutrients, particularly iron, of the various grades of molasses. Although molasses is usually consumed in small amounts, it is a good source of the minerals calcium, magnesium, potassium, and iron. Molasses adds a nice flavoring to breads, cakes, and cookies and helps maintain the freshness of baked products. Molasses is frequently used in baked bean recipes and as a glaze for sweet potatoes.

Onion Soup Bread

Turned out as a heavy "loaf"

Everyone loves this richly flavored, aromatic bread — a party favorite.

1-pound loaf (8 – 10 servings):
$2/3$ cup water
2 teaspoons canola oil
1 $1/2$ tablespoons molasses
$1/2$ packet onion soup mix
$1/3$ cup cornmeal
1 $3/4$ cups (9.5 ounces) whole wheat flour
1 $1/2$ tablespoons gluten flour
1 tablespoon powdered whey
1 $1/2$ teaspoons active dry yeast

1 $1/2$-pound loaf (12 – 14 servings):
1 $1/8$ cups water
1 tablespoon canola oil
2 tablespoons molasses
1 packet onion soup mix
$1/2$ cup cornmeal
2 $1/4$ cups (12.2 ounces) whole wheat flour
2 tablespoons gluten flour
1 $1/2$ tablespoons powdered whey
2 teaspoons active dry yeast

Put the ingredients in the bread pan in the order listed, or in the reverse order if the manual for your machine calls for dry ingredients first and liquids last. Select Basic Wheat Cycle, Light Setting (or the equivalent setting for your machine). Push Start.

Nutrient Analysis per Serving:
Calories: 119
Carbohydrates: 23
Protein: 4
Fat: 2
Fiber: 4

RECIPE TIP

If you are watching your sodium intake, use a low-sodium onion soup mix.

Tomatoes

Tomatoes were first domesticated in Mexico and were later introduced in Europe by Columbus. Although the English colonists brought tomato seeds to the New World, the tomato did not become popular until the latter part of the nineteenth century. It has since grown steadily in prominence. Tomatoes are now available in several varieties, including firmer, squarish types that can be harvested by machines and genetically engineered varieties.

Tomatoes are available fresh, canned, as tomato sauce, or as tomato paste. Tomato paste is made from deseeded, strained tomato pulp, concentrated to yield 4 times more solids than tomato juice. Salt and baking soda are often added, the latter to neutralize natural acids. Tomato paste is a concentrated source of nutrients; it is rich in pro-vitamin A and vitamin K, as well as several other vitamins and some minerals. Never store leftover tomato paste in its original can. Exposed to oxygen, the metals in the can react with and break down the vitamins and minerals in the paste.

Tomato Bread

A great complement to your favorite pasta dish.

1-pound loaf (8 – 10 servings):

3/4 cup water
1 teaspoon olive oil
1 teaspoon honey
1/2 6-ounce can tomato paste
3/4 teaspoon salt
2 tablespoons powdered egg substitute
1/3 cup cornmeal
1 1/3 cups (7.2 ounces) whole wheat flour
1/2 cup (2.6 ounces) unbleached flour
1 1/2 tablespoons gluten flour
1 teaspoon garlic powder
1 teaspoon dried basil
1/2 teaspoon pepper
1 tablespoon powdered whey
1 1/2 teaspoons active dry yeast

1 1/2-pound loaf (12 – 14 servings):

1 cup plus 3 tablespoons water
1 1/2 teaspoons olive oil
1 1/2 teaspoons honey
1 6-ounce can tomato paste
1 teaspoon salt
3 tablespoons powdered egg substitute
1/2 cup cornmeal
2 cups (10.8 ounces) whole wheat flour
3/4 cup (3.9 ounces) unbleached flour
2 tablespoons gluten flour
1 1/2 teaspoons garlic powder
1 1/2 teaspoons dried basil
1 teaspoon pepper
1 1/2 tablespoons powdered whey
2 teaspoons active dry yeast

Follow the instructions for other breads in this chapter.

Nutrient Analysis per Serving:
Calories: 116
Carbohydrates: 23
Protein: 5

Fat: 1
Fiber: 3

Oregano

Oregano is one of the world's most popular herbs. It is a standard in Italian cooking for seasoning tomato sauces and is commonly used in omelets, yeast breads, and vegetable and meat dishes. Its hot, peppery flavor combines well with garlic, thyme, parsley, and olive oil.

Most of oregano's early uses were medicinal, not culinary. Ground oregano has been used to make poultices for sore and aching muscles. As a tea, oregano has been used for chronic coughs and asthma, for indigestion, to relieve intestinal gas, and as a tonic. The aroma of the flowers reportedly helps to relieve seasickness.

Oregano only caught on in North American cooking after World War II, when servicemen returned home with a taste for Mediterranean cooking. Though spaghetti was well known in the U.S., it took the widespread appeal of pizza to firmly establish oregano as all-American.

Pizza Bread

Mama mia! — a meal in itself.

1-pound loaf (8 – 10 servings).

1 cup pizza sauce
1 tablespoon olive oil
1/2 cup "mozzarella" soy cheese, grated
1/3 cup mushrooms, diced
3/4 teaspoon salt
2 tablespoons dried tomatoes, diced
1 1/2 tablespoons dried onions
1 1/3 cups (7.2 ounces) whole wheat flour
2/3 cup (3.5 ounces) unbleached flour
2/3 teaspoon oregano
1 1/2 teaspoons active dry yeast

1 1/2-pound loaf (12 – 14 servings):

1 1/2 cups pizza sauce
1 1/2 tablespoons olive oil
2/3 cup "mozzarella" soy cheese, grated
1/2 cup mushrooms, diced
1 1/4 teaspoons salt
1/4 cup dried tomatoes, diced
2 tablespoons dried onions
2 cups (10.8 ounces) whole wheat flour
1 cup (5.2 ounces) unbleached flour
1 teaspoon oregano
2 teaspoons active dry yeast

Put the ingredients in the bread pan in the order listed, or in the reverse order if the manual for your machine calls for dry ingredients first and liquids last. Select Basic Wheat Cycle, Light Setting (or the equivalent setting for your machine). Push Start.

RECIPE TIP

Because of the different consistencies of pizza sauces, you may need to add a little water to this recipe.

Nutrient Analysis per Serving:
Calories: 175
Carbohydrates: 26
Protein: 7
Fat: 3
Fiber: 2

103

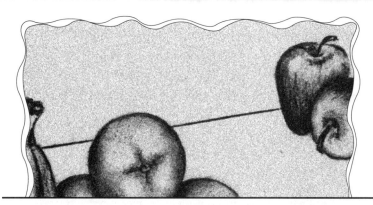

CHAPTER SEVEN

Fruit Breads and Sweet Breads

Oranges

First introduced to Florida by Spanish explorers in the mid-1500s, oranges are now the leading fruit crop in the U.S. and are grown in both Florida and California. They are the third largest fruit crop in the world, falling only behind grapes and bananas. Though known by their characteristic bright orange color, color is actually not a good indicator of maturity. Oranges only turn orange when exposed to cool night temperatures; most oranges are picked green and then exposed to ethylene gas in a warm room to turn them an orange color.

For health and nutrition, it's hard to beat the great taste of fresh oranges and orange juice. Oranges are naturally low in calories and a good source of fiber, pectin, potassium, vitamin C, inositol, and bioflavinoids (vitamin-like substances) nd are a fair source of folic acid. Drinking range juice with meals is an easy way to substan- ally boost your iron absorption from plant foods — as much as 400 percent! Thus vegetarians, or anyone seeking to boost the iron content of their diet, should always choose fresh orange juice or oranges over canned juices. (Canned juices are heat pasteurized, a process that greatly depletes that vitamin C and folic acid content of fruits.)

Orange Spice Bread

Try this zesty combination of citrus and spices.

1-pound loaf (8 – 10 servings):

1/2 cup water
2 teaspoons canola oil
1/3 cup orange juice
2 teaspoons fructose
1 1/2 teaspoons orange marmalade
1/2 teaspoon lemon zest
2/3 teaspoon salt
1 cup (5.4 ounces) whole wheat flour
1 cup (5.2 ounces) unbleached flour
1 1/2 tablespoons gluten flour
1 1/2 teaspoons cinnamon
1 1/2 tablespoons powdered whey
1 1/2 teaspoons active dry yeast

1 1/2-pound loaf (12 – 14 servings):

2/3 cup water
1 tablespoon canola oil
1/2 cup orange juice
1 tablespoon fructose
2 tablespoons orange marmalade
1 teaspoon lemon zest
1 teaspoon salt
1 1/2 cups (8.1 ounces) whole wheat flour
1 1/2 cups (7.8 ounces) unbleached flour
2 tablespoons gluten flour
2 teaspoons cinnamon
2 tablespoons powdered whey
2 teaspoons active dry yeast

Put the ingredients in the bread pan in the order listed, or in the reverse order if the manual for your machine calls for dry ingredients first and liquids last. Select Basic Wheat Cycle, Light Setting (or the equivalent setting for your machine). Push Start.

Nutrient Analysis per Serving:
Calories: 127
Carbohydrates: 26
Protein: 4
Fat: 1
Fiber: 2

Bananas

It is believed that bananas originated in Malaysia approximately 4,000 years ago. From there, they spread to India, the Philippines, and New Guinea. Bananas are not a commercial crop in the United States; most of the bananas we buy are imported from Central and South America. The most popular type of banana is the large yellow, smooth-skinned variety. This banana is known as the Manque or Gros Michel (Big Mike). Fresh bananas are packed full of nutrients, providing an excellent source of natural sugars and many vitamins and minerals, especially potassium. A medium-size banana contains approximately 100 calories and 2.3 grams of fiber.

Fresh bananas are best when the peel is a bright yellow with some brown spots but is still firm. Green tips with no brown spots means the banana has not been fully ripened and therefore lacks its full flavor. Bananas should have no bruises. They will continue ripening at room temperature as their starch hydrolizes to sugars, producing their familiar sweetness. In the refrigerator, bananas remain fresh for 3 to 5 days, although the peel will become very dark.

Banana Nut Bread

Banana chips make this an all-around favorite.

1 pound loaf (8 – 10 servings):
2/3 cup water
1 tablespoon canola oil
1 tablespoon honey
1 tablespoon banana flavoring
1 teaspoon salt
1 1/2 cups (8.1 ounces) whole wheat flour
1/2 cup (2.6 ounces) unbleached flour
2 teaspoons gluten flour
1/8 cup chopped walnuts
1/8 cup banana chips
4 teaspoons powdered whey
1 1/2 teaspoons active dry yeast

1 1/2-pound loaf (12 – 14 servings):
1 cup plus 3 tablespoons water
1 1/2 tablespoons canola oil
1 1/2 tablespoons honey
1 1/2 tablespoons banana flavoring
1 1/2 teaspoons salt
2 cups (10.8 ounces) whole wheat flour
1 cup (5.2 ounces) unbleached flour
1 tablespoon gluten flour
1/4 cup chopped walnuts
1/4 cup banana chips
2 tablespoons powdered whey
2 teaspoons active dry yeast

Put the ingredients in the bread pan in the order listed, or in the reverse order if the manual for your machine calls for dry ingredients first and liquids last. Select Basic Wheat Cycle, Light Setting (or the equivalent setting for your machine). Push Start.

Nutrient Analysis per Serving:
Calories: 169
Carbohydrates: 22
Protein: 5
Fat: 5
Fiber: 3

Apricots

Apricots first originated in China, and it is thought that Alexander the Great brought them to Greece. The fruit of the apricot tree is classified as a drupe. A drupe is a 1-seeded fruit that does not split open on its own. Closely related to the almond, cherry, peach, and plum, apricots are orange or yellow in color and have a smooth, sweet flesh.

Apricot trees grow in various areas throughout the United States and are sold fresh, canned, dried, and frozen. They can also be added to fruit dishes or made into jams, pies, and puddings. Dried apricots make a deliciously chewy, healthy snack and are a good source of beta-carotene, potassium, and iron.

When purchasing dried apricots, choose those that are unsulphured (sulphur dioxide is commonly used in dried fruit to prevent browning). Sulfites can cause allergic reactions in sensitive individuals, and the only real benefits sulphuring provides are a lighter product and a softer texture. Nonsulphured, or sun-dried, fruit is by far a healthier choice and can be easily softened by first wrapping the fruit in a moistened paper towel, placing it in a plastic bag, then storing it in the refrigerator. Be aware that storing dried fruit in the refrigerator can accelerate sugaring, the migration of natural sugars within the fruit to the surface. When this occurs, the fruit might look like it has tiny white crystals on the surface, which are actually sugars, not mold, but which some people mistake for mold and so unnecessarily throw out the fruit.

Apricot Bread

Sweet and tangy — a real winner.

1-pound loaf (8 – 10 servings):

$3/4$ cup water
1 tablespoon canola oil
1 $1/2$ tablespoons honey
1 teaspoon salt
$1/2$ cup oats
1 cup (5.4 ounces) whole wheat flour
$1/2$ cup (2.6 ounces) unbleached flour
2 tablespoons chopped almonds
$1/4$ cup diced dried apricots
2 tablespoons powdered whey
1 $1/2$ teaspoons active dry yeast

1 $1/2$-pound loaf (12 – 14 servings):

1 cup plus 2 tablespoons water
1 $1/2$ tablespoons canola oil
2 tablespoons honey
1 $1/2$ teaspoons salt
$3/4$ cup oats
1 $1/2$ cups (8.1 ounces) whole wheat flour
$3/4$ cup (3.9 ounces) unbleached flour
$1/4$ cup chopped almonds
$1/3$ cup diced dried apricots
3 tablespoons powdered whey
2 teaspoons active dry yeast

RECIPE TIP

For a lowfat version, leave out the nuts; this will reduce the fat approximately 1 gram per serving. For variety, try other dried fruits such as cranberries.

Put the ingredients in the bread pan in the order listed, or in the reverse order if the manual for your machine calls for dry ingredients first and liquids last. Select Basic Wheat Cycle, Light Setting (or the equivalent setting for your machine). Push Start.

Nutrient Analysis per Serving:
Calories: 153
Carbohydrates: 26
Protein: 5
Fat: 4
Fiber: 2

Cinnamon

Cinnamon is native to Sri Lanka, India, and Malaysia and has a long history. Egyptians used cinnamon in their embalming mixtures. Later, the desire for cinnamon and other spices spurred world exploration. Although the evergreen bush or tree from which cinnamon is derived can grow to heights of 30 feet, the cultivated tree is kept pruned to shrub height for ease of harvesting. Cinnamon is produced from the inner bark. As it dries, it curls into the characteristic sticks sold whole in spice jars. Cinnamon complements the spices vanilla, nutmeg, fennel, ginger, clove, and cardamom.

Cinnamon has its own unique medicinal history. It has long been used in both Eastern and Western cultures as a medicine and folk remedy for arthritis, asthma, cancer, diarrhea, fever, heart problems, insomnia, menstrual problems, peptic ulcers, psoriasis, and spastic muscles. Scientific studies have confirmed the beneficial effects of cinnamon as a sedative, anti-convulsant, diuretic, antibiotic, and anti-ulcerative agent. It also destroys the fungi that produce aflatoxin, a potent carcinogen and poison sometimes found in peanuts.

Cinnamon Raisin Bread

good

An all-time favorite—tastes great piping hot on a cold winter morning.

1-pound loaf (8 – 10 servings):
- 3/4 cup plus 1 tablespoon water
- 1 tablespoon canola oil
- 1 tablespoon brown sugar
- 1/3 teaspoon salt
- 1 1/3 cups (7.2 ounces) whole wheat flour
- 1/2 cup (2.6 ounces) unbleached flour
- 2 tablespoons gluten flour
- 1/2 teaspoon cinnamon
- 1/3 cup raisins
- 1 tablespoon powdered whey
- 1 1/2 teaspoons active dry yeast

RECIPE TIP

Some machines suggest adding raisins halfway through the kneading cycle. Be sure to follow the instructions for your machine.

1 1/2-pound loaf (12 – 14 servings):
- 1 1/4 cups water
- 1 1/2 tablespoons canola oil
- 1 1/2 tablespoons brown sugar
- 1/2 teaspoon salt
- 2 cups (10.8 ounces) whole wheat flour
- 3/4 cup (3.9 ounces) unbleached flour
- 3 tablespoons gluten flour
- 3/4 teaspoon cinnamon
- 1/2 cup raisins
- 1 1/2 tablespoons powdered whey
- 2 teaspoons active dry yeast

+ 1 T wheat germ
+ 1 T oat bran
+ 1 T wheat bran

Put the ingredients in the bread pan in the order listed, or in the reverse order if the manual for your machine calls for dry ingredients first and liquids last. Select Basic Wheat Cycle, Light Setting (or the equivalent setting for your machine). Push Start.

Nutrient Analysis per Serving:
Calories: 127
Carbohydrates: 25
Protein: 4

Fat: 2
Fiber: 3

113

Apples

The apple originated in the Caucasus mountains of Western Asia and was spread by the Greeks and Romans, who cultivated apples when they took over England and other areas of Europe. First introduced to North America during the early 1620s, apples were gradually spread by explorers, Native Americans, and pioneers, especially a man named John Chapman (known to most of us as Johnny Appleseed). Today, more than 25 varieties of apples are available in the United States.

Apples are a good source of pectin, a type of fiber that provides a number of beneficial health effects. Because it is a gel-forming fiber, pectin improves the intestinal muscle's ability to push waste through the gastrointestinal tract. Pectin also helps to lower cholesterol levels.

Applesauce Walnut Bread

The recipe all your neighbors will ask for.

1 pound loaf (8 - 10 servings):

$1/2$ cup apple juice
2 teaspoons canola oil
1 tablespoon honey
$1/2$ teaspoon vanilla
2 $1/2$ tablespoons nonfat yogurt
$1/3$ cup applesauce
$1/3$ cup chopped apple
1 teaspoon salt
1 $1/2$ cups (8.1 ounces) whole wheat flour
$3/4$ cup (3.9 ounces) unbleached flour
$1/4$ cup walnuts
1 $1/2$ teaspoons active dry yeast

1 $1/2$-pound loaf (12 – 14 servings):

$3/4$ cup apple juice
1 tablespoon canola oil
1 $1/2$ tablespoons honey
$2/3$ teaspoon vanilla
$1/4$ cup nonfat yogurt
$1/2$ cup applesauce
$1/2$ cup chopped apple
1 $1/2$ teaspoons salt
2 $1/4$ cups (12.2 ounces) whole wheat flour
1 $1/4$ cups (6.5 ounces) unbleached flour
$1/3$ cup walnuts
2 teaspoons active dry yeast

RECIPE TIP

This recipe may need a little help from your spatula to get it all mixed together properly. Be sure to watch for proper dough consistency during the kneading cycle.

Put the ingredients in the bread pan in the order listed, or in the reverse order if the manual for your machine calls for dry ingredients first and liquids last. Select Basic Wheat Cycle, Light Setting (or the equivalent setting for your machine). Push Start.

Nutrient Analysis per Serving:
Calories: 150
Carbohydrates: 26
Protein: 5

Fat: 4
Fiber: 3

Maple Syrup

The sugar maple tree that grows in New England and Canada, particularly in the province of Quebec, produces a sweet sap that is boiled and reduced to a delightful syrup. It takes from 35 to 50 gallons of sap to make 1 gallon of pure maple syrup, which helps to explain its cost. Pure maple syrup contains about 50 calories per tablespoon along with some calcium and potassium. Most commercial brands of pancake syrup contain little pure maple syrup and high amounts of corn syrup as well as sugar, honey, molasses, fruit juice, caramel color, chemical emulsifiers, acidifiers, defoaming agents, preservatives, salt, and artificial flavors. Log Cabin Syrup, for example, used to contain 45 percent maple syrup, but now contains only 3 percent. Like all liquid sweeteners, maple syrup attracts moisture, keeping baked goods fresher longer. To prevent mold or fermentation, store pure maple syrup in your refrigerator. Because maple sugar is sweeter than table sugar, substitute 2/3 to 3/4 cup of maple syrup for 1 cup of granulated sugar.

Fry
V. good

Maple Syrup Bread

Tastes just like french toast. An excellent breakfast bread.

1-pound loaf (8–10 servings):
2/3 cup water
1 tablespoon canola oil
1/3 cup maple syrup
2/3 teaspoon salt
2/3 cup wheat flakes
1 cup (5.4 ounces) whole wheat flour
2/3 cup (3.5 ounces) unbleached flour
2 tablespoons gluten flour
1 tablespoon powdered whey
1 1/2 teaspoons active dry yeast

1 1/2-pound loaf (12–14 servings):
1 cup water
1 1/2 tablespoons canola oil
1/2 cup maple syrup
1 teaspoon salt
1 cup wheat flakes
1 1/2 cups (8.1 ounces) whole wheat flour
1 cup (5.2 ounces) unbleached flour
3 tablespoons gluten flour
1 1/2 tablespoons powdered whey
2 teaspoons active dry yeast

Put the ingredients in the bread pan in the order listed, or in the reverse order if the manual for your machine calls for dry ingredients first and liquids last. Select Basic Wheat Cycle, Light Setting (or the equivalent setting for your machine). Push Start.

Nutrient Analysis per Serving:
Calories: 136
Carbohydrates: 27
Protein: 4
Fat: 2
Fiber: 3

Yeast

Yeast are tiny, 1-celled fungi that feed on plant sugars and are used as a leavening agent to cause bread to rise. (However, yeast-free breads can be made for people allergic to yeast.) Yeast is also commonly used in pizzas, crackers, and certain cakes.

Although there are about 350 different species of yeast, the most common kind used as a leavener in baking is active dry yeast. This yeast is sold in small packets that contain approximately a tablespoon of yeast. Active dry yeast is alive but dormant. When provided with warmth, moisture, and food, it begins to grow and multiply, giving off carbon dioxide as a by-product of its activity. It is this carbon dioxide gas that catches in the gluten strands and causes bread to rise.

Yeast can also be purchased in the form of a small, solid cake that can be kept in the refrigerator for up to 2 weeks or stored in the freezer for 2 months. Active dry yeast, in contrast, can be stored in the refrigerator for many months. An expiration date is stamped on each packet. Be sure to check the expiration date before using, because old yeast will not lift the bread to the desired height. You can proof the yeast using the following simple method:

Put 1 teaspoon of sugar and 1 tablespoon of yeast in a liquid measuring container with a 1/2 cup of warm water. After 3 to 4 minutes, if the water level has risen to the 1 cup level, the yeast is active.

Maple Oat Bread

V good

An oatmeal variation of the basic Maple Syrup Bread.

1-pound loaf (8 – 10 servings):

$2/3$ cup water
1 tablespoon canola oil
$1/3$ cup maple syrup
$2/3$ teaspoon salt
$1/2$ cup rolled oats
1 cup (5.4 ounces) whole wheat flour
$2/3$ cup (3.5 ounces) unbleached flour
2 tablespoons gluten flour
1 tablespoon powdered whey
1 $1/2$ teaspoons active dry yeast

1 $1/2$-pound loaf (12 – 14 servings):

1 $1/8$ cups water
1 $1/2$ tablespoons canola oil
$2/3$ cup maple syrup
1 teaspoon salt
$3/4$ cup rolled oats
1 $1/2$ cups (8.1 ounces) whole wheat flour
1 cup (5.2 ounces) unbleached flour
3 tablespoons gluten flour
1 $1/2$ tablespoons powdered whey
2 teaspoons active dry yeast

Put the ingredients in the bread pan in the order listed, or in the reverse order if the manual for your machine calls for dry ingredients first and liquids last. Select Basic Wheat Cycle, Light Setting (or the equivalent setting for your machine). Push Start.

Nutrient Analysis per Serving:
Calories: 132
Carbohydrates: 29
Protein: 4
Fat: 2
Fiber: 2

Cranberries

In the United States, cranberries were first cultivated in Massachusetts by Dennis Hall, who noticed that the berries grew well under certain climate conditions in his bog. Today, most of the world cranberry crop is produced in the United States in swampy, low-lying acid bogs. The crop is processed into fruit drinks or cranberry sauces or frozen whole for future processing into these products or for sale in grocery freezers.

Cranberry Amaranth Bread

An ancient grain alternative to a traditional holiday treat to be enjoyed at any time of the year.

1-pound loaf (8 – 10 servings):
2/3 cup water
1 tablespoon canola oil
2 tablespoons honey
2/3 teaspoon salt
1/2 cup amaranth flour
1 cup (5.4 ounces) whole wheat flour
1/2 cup (2.6 ounces) unbleached flour
1/3 cup dried cranberries
1 tablespoon powdered whey
1 1/2 teaspoons active dry yeast

1 1/2-pound loaf (12 – 14 servings):
1 cup water
1 1/2 tablespoons canola oil
3 tablespoons honey
1 teaspoon salt
3/4 cup amaranth flour
1 1/2 cups (8.1 ounces) whole wheat flour
2/3 cup (3.5 ounces) unbleached flour
1/2 cup dried cranberries
1 1/2 tablespoons powdered whey
2 1/2 teaspoons active dry yeast

Put the ingredients in the bread pan in the order listed, or in the reverse order if the manual for your machine calls for dry ingredients first and liquids last. Select Basic Wheat Cycle, Light Setting (or the equivalent setting for your machine). Push Start.

Nutrient Analysis per Serving:
Calories: 103
Carbohydrates: 21
Protein: 3
Fat: 2
Fiber: 2

Vegetable Oils

Vegetable oils are fats that are in liquid form at room temperature. Medical experts recommend we increase the monounsaturated-to-polyunsaturated fat ratio in our diets to help lower blood cholesterol levels and to reduce the risk of heart disease. Oils rich in monounsaturated fats, such as olive and canola oils, appear to be the most effective in reducing cholesterol levels. Remember, no oil is 100% unsaturated; corn, soybean, safflower, and other kinds of oil all contain some saturated fat. In fact, some of the tropical oils, such as coconut and palm kernel oil, contain more saturated fat than many animal products. As a general rule, the higher the ratio of unsaturated to saturated fatty acids, the healthier the fat.

All oils contain about 14 grams of fat and 120 calories per tablespoon and are the richest dietary source of the fat-soluble vitamin E. All fats, including oils, should be used sparingly in a health-promoting diet. Current recommendations urge us to cut our total fat intake to no more than 30 percent of daily calories (15 – 20 percent would be even better). Our national average for fat intake now stands at 37 percent — much higher than is healthy.

Cranberry Wheat Bread

Good

Visually interesting, and delicious as well!

1-pound loaf (8 – 10 servings):

$3/4$ cup water
1 tablespoon canola oil
2 tablespoons honey
$3/4$ teaspoon salt
1 $1/3$ cups (7.2 ounces) whole wheat flour
$2/3$ cup (3.5 ounces) unbleached flour
$1/3$ cup dried cranberries
1 tablespoon powdered whey
1 $1/2$ teaspoons active dry yeast

1 $1/2$-pound loaf (12 – 14 servings):

1 $1/8$ cups water
1 $1/2$ tablespoons canola oil
3 tablespoons honey
1 teaspoon salt
2 cups (10.8 ounces) whole wheat flour
1 cup (5.2 ounces) unbleached flour
$1/2$ cup dried cranberries
1 $1/2$ tablespoons powdered whey
2 teaspoons active dry yeast

Put the ingredients in the bread pan in the order listed, or in the reverse order if the manual for your machine calls for dry ingredients first and liquids last. Select Basic Wheat Cycle, Light Setting (or the equivalent setting for your machine). Push Start.

Nutrient Analysis per Serving:
Calories: 127
Carbohydrates: 26
Protein: 4
Fat: 2
Fiber: 3

Oats

Oats are among the most recently cultivated cereal grasses and can be found rolled, flaked, steel-cut, or as groats. Regular rolled oats are used to make oatmeal but can also be used for baking cookies, muffins, and quick breads. Oats are 10 to 15 percent protein, and because only the inedible hull is removed when oats are milled, oats offer a good source of fiber and B vitamins as well as respectable amounts of iron, magnesium, zinc, potassium, manganese, calcium, and copper. Despite the fact that they have a slightly higher fat content than other grains, oats are low in calories (1 cup contains only 130 calories) and quite filling. Oats naturally contain cafeic acid derivatives and anti-oxidants that delay rancidity. This explains why properly processed oatmeal is extremely shelf-stable and can be maintained in closed containers for many years.

Only about 55 percent of all the oats grown in the United States are intended for human consumption. Most are fed to animals, even though over 20 clinical studies since 1963 suggest that adding oats or oat bran to the diet can lower high blood cholesterol levels, especially when consumed in conjunction with a low-fat diet. A mere 1/2 cup a day of oat bran can help lower blood cholesterol by up to 20 percent.

Apple and Oat Bread

A scrumptious breakfast delight.

1-pound loaf (8 – 10 servings):
- $1/2$ cup water
- 1 tablespoon canola oil
- 1 tablespoon honey
- 1 teaspoon molasses
- $1/2$ cup chopped apples
- 2 teaspoons lemon juice
- 2 tablespoons nonfat yogurt
- 1 teaspoon salt
- $1/2$ cup oats
- 1 $1/3$ cups (7.2 ounces) whole wheat flour
- $2/3$ cup (3.5 ounces) unbleached flour
- 1 teaspoon cinnamon
- 2 teaspoons powdered whey
- 1 $1/2$ teaspoons active dry yeast

1 $1/2$-pound loaf (12 – 14 servings):
- $3/4$ cup water
- 1 $1/2$ tablespoons canola oil
- 2 tablespoons honey
- 1 tablespoon molasses
- $3/4$ cup chopped apples
- 1 tablespoon lemon juice
- $1/4$ cup nonfat yogurt
- 1 $1/2$ teaspoons salt
- $3/4$ cup oats
- 2 cups (10.8 ounces) whole wheat flour
- 1 cup (5.2 ounces) unbleached flour
- 1 $1/2$ teaspoons cinnamon
- 1 tablespoon powdered whey
- 2 $1/4$ teaspoons active dry yeast

Put the ingredients in the bread pan in the order listed, or in the reverse order if the manual for your machine calls for dry ingredients first and liquids last. Select Basic Wheat Cycle, Light Setting (or the equivalent setting for your machine). Push Start.

Nutrient Analysis per Serving:

Calories: 153	*Fat: 3*
Carbohydrates: 29	*Fiber: 3*
Protein: 5	

125

Berries

Berries are rich in vital nutrients yet low in calories. This combination makes them excellent foods for individuals with a "sweet tooth" who are attempting to improve the quality of their nutrition without increasing the caloric content of their diet. Berries have long been used for a wide range of medicinal effects, and current research is providing scientific support for many of the folk uses of berries. For example, during World War II, British Royal Air Force pilots consumed bilberry (a variety of blueberry) preserves before their night missions. The pilots believed folk medicine tales that the bilberries would improve their ability to see at night. After the war, numerous studies demonstrated that bilberry extracts do in fact improve nighttime visual acuity and lead to quicker adjustment to darkness as well as faster restoration of visual acuity after exposure to glare.

Berry Bread

Berry berry good!

1-pound loaf (8 – 10 servings)

1/3 cup water
1 tablespoon canola oil
1 tablespoon honey
2/3 cup fresh blueberries or raspberries
1/3 teaspoon salt
1 cup (5.4 ounces) whole wheat flour
2/3 cup (3.5 ounces) unbleached flour
1/3 cup chopped nuts
1 1/2 teaspoons active dry yeast

1 1/2-pound loaf (12 – 14 servings):

1/2 cup water
1 1/2 tablespoons canola oil
1 1/2 tablespoons honey
1 cup fresh blueberries or raspberries
1/2 teaspoon salt
1 1/2 cups (8.1 ounces) whole wheat flour
1 cup (5.2 ounces) unbleached flour
1/2 cup chopped nuts
2 teaspoons active dry yeast

Put the ingredients in the bread pan in the order listed, or in the reverse order if the manual for your machine calls for dry ingredients first and liquids last. Select Basic Wheat Cycle, Light Setting (or the equivalent setting for your machine). Push Start.

Nutrient Analysis per Serving:
Calories: 110
Carbohydrates: 21
Protein: 3
Fat: 2
Fiber: 3

RECIPE TIP

This bread can be tricky! Because of the variation in the moisture content of fresh berries, the liquid portion of the recipe may have to be adjusted each time.

Carob

Carob is made from the roasted and ground fruit pods of a Mediterranean evergreen tree. Originally native to the Middle East, carob is also known as St. John's bread, locust bean, and locust pod. These names derive from the belief that carob pods were the ones referred to in the Bible (Matthew 3:4) as the "locusts" that St. John ate with honey while traveling in the desert.

Interest in carob for use as an alternative to chocolate began in the 1920s. Naturally sweet, it is used as a substitute for cocoa in baked goods, chocolate chips, candy, hot chocolate — any item that uses cocoa. Carob is low in fat and provides about 8 percent protein plus B vitamins, calcium, and magnesium. For cooking, carob is a healthier choice than chocolate for several reasons. Its mild flavor is naturally sweeter and less bitter than baker's chocolate; it contains more healthful nutrients than chocolate and does not contain caffeine or theobromine, two stimulants common to both chocolate and coffee that speed up the heartbeat and stimulate the central nervous system. Carob is also free of the oxalic acid found in chocolate, which can interfere with calcium absorption when used excessively.

Peanut Butter Carob Bread

Seems too decadent to be healthy — but it is!!

1-pound loaf (8 – 10 servings):

3/4 cup water
2 tablespoons Sucanat™
1/3 cup peanut butter
1/4 teaspoon salt
1 cup (5.4 ounces) whole wheat flour
1 cup (5.2 ounces) unbleached flour
2 tablespoons gluten flour
1/3 cup carob chips
1 tablespoon powdered whey
2 teaspoons active dry yeast

1 1/2-pound loaf (12 – 14 servings):

1 1/4 cups water
3 tablespoons Sucanat™
1/2 cup peanut butter
1/2 teaspoon salt
1 1/2 cups (8.1 ounces) whole wheat flour
1 1/2 cups (7.8 ounces) unbleached flour
3 tablespoons gluten flour
1/2 cup carob chips
2 tablespoons powdered whey
3 teaspoons active dry yeast

Put the ingredients in the bread pan in the order listed, or in the reverse order if the manual for your machine calls for dry ingredients first and liquids last. Select Basic Wheat Cycle, Light Setting (or the equivalent setting for your machine). Push Start.

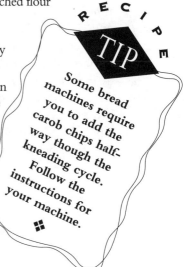

RECIPE TIP

Some bread machines require you to add the carob chips half-way though the kneading cycle. Follow the instructions for your machine.

Nutrient Analysis per Serving:
Calories: 212
Carbohydrates: 28
Protein: 8
Fat: 7
Fiber: 3

Vanilla

Vanilla is the pod of a climbing orchid native to the humid forests of the Americas and has been used as a flavoring for many centuries. It was brought to Europe by the Spanish explorers, who observed the Aztecs use it as a flavoring for chocolate. Today, it is mostly used in sweet dishes, such as bakery products or desserts. Fresh vanilla pods have no flavor; the flavor develops only as a result of internal chemical activity (enzymatic reactions) during the curing process.

The flavor of vanilla pods is definitely superior to the essence. The pods can also be used many times over, provided they are washed afterward and redried. The best vanilla essence is made from crushing the vanilla pods and then adding alcohol. Many vanilla extracts may not be as pure as they seem; it is common practice to include dextrose, sugar, corn syrup, propylene glycol, and glycerin without revealing any of these on the label. When you purchase vanilla flavoring, make sure the label says "pure vanilla extract."

Banana Wheat Bread

A wholesome, moist bread bursting with banana flavor.

Try
food — a basic
whole wheat type
with touch of
banana + extra
moist +

1-pound loaf (8 – 10 servings):
- 3/4 cup water
- 2 teaspoons canola oil
- 1 1/2 tablespoons honey
- 1/8 teaspoon vanilla
- 1 1/2 bananas, sliced
- 1/2 teaspoon salt
- 1 cup (5.4 ounces) whole wheat flour
- 3/4 cup (3.9 ounces) unbleached flour
- 1 tablespoon gluten flour
- 1 1/2 tablespoons powdered whey
- 1 1/2 teaspoons active dry yeast

Using frozen bananas is way too much liquid — had to add a lot of extra flour

1 1/2-pound loaf (12 – 14 servings):
- 1 1/8 cups water
- 1 tablespoon canola oil
- 2 tablespoons honey
- 1/4 teaspoon vanilla
- 2 bananas, sliced
- 1 teaspoon salt
- 1 1/2 cups (8.1 ounces) whole wheat flour
- 1 1/4 cups (6.5 ounces) unbleached flour
- 2 tablespoons gluten flour
- 2 tablespoons powdered whey
- 3 teaspoons active dry yeast

Put the ingredients in the bread pan in the order listed, or in the reverse order if the manual for your machine calls for dry ingredients first and liquids last. Select Basic Wheat Cycle, Light Setting (or the equivalent setting for your machine). Push Start.

Nutrient Analysis per Serving:
Calories: 131
Carbohydrates: 26
Protein: 4
Fat: 2
Fiber: 3

Dates

The date palm is considered to be the first cultivated tree in history, and mature trees can achieve a height of up to 100 feet. Dates grow in clusters containing up to 200 fruits and weighing up to 25 pounds. Native to the Middle East and North Africa, dates remain an important food in these areas. About 75 percent of the world's date crop is grown in the Middle East, but most of the United States' supply comes from California and Arizona.

Ounce for ounce, dates supply 64 percent more potassium than a banana, but they also contain about 60 percent more calories. Dates are one of the sweetest fruits, containing up to 70 percent sugar.

Date Walnut Crunch Bread

A wholesome loaf, bursting with different flavors and textures!

1-pound loaf (8 – 10 servings):
3/4 cup plus 1 tablespoon water
2 teaspoons canola oil
2 teaspoons honey
1/2 tablespoon molasses
1 teaspoon salt
1 cup (5.4 ounces) whole wheat flour
2/3 cup (3.5 ounces) unbleached flour
1/3 cup fat-free granola
1/3 cup dates, chopped
1/3 cup walnuts, chopped
2 tablespoons powdered whey
1 1/2 teaspoons active dry yeast

1 1/2-pound loaf (12 – 14 servings):
1 1/4 cups water
1 tablespoon canola oil
1 tablespoon honey
1 tablespoon molasses
1 1/2 teaspoons salt
1 1/2 cups (8.1 ounces) whole wheat flour
1 cup (5.2 ounces) unbleached flour
1/2 cup fat-free granola
1/2 cup dates, chopped
1/2 cup walnuts, chopped
3 tablespoons powdered whey
2 teaspoons active dry yeast

Put the ingredients in the bread pan in the order listed, or in the reverse order if the manual for your machine calls for dry ingredients first and liquids last. Select Basic Wheat Cycle, Light Setting (or the equivalent setting for your machine). Push Start.

Nutrient Analysis per Serving:
Calories: 161
Carbohydrates: 27
Protein: 5
Fat: 5
Fiber: 3

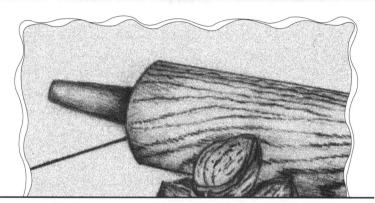

CHAPTER EIGHT

Nut and Seed Breads

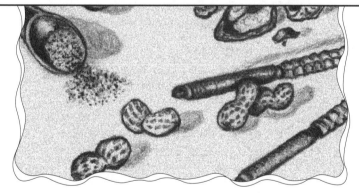

Nuts

Nuts, along with seeds, are the vehicle for plant reproduction. Locked inside each nut is the potential for an entire new plant. Nuts and seeds are nutritious; they are especially good sources of essential fatty acids, vitamin E, protein, and minerals. Purchase your nuts and seeds whole; they'll keep longer. It takes surprisingly little time to shell the small amount of nuts required in most recipes. When you buy whole nuts, make sure the shells are free from splits, cracks, stains, holes, or other surface imperfections. Store nuts and seeds in their shells in a cool, dry environment. If whole nuts and seeds in their shells are not available, make sure the shelled ones you purchase are vacuum-packed or stored in air-tight containers in a refrigerator or freezer.

Of the many varieties of nuts, it's amusing that the most popular nut is the peanut, which is actually not a nut at all but a legume. The peanut is also unusual in that it begins as an aboveground flower that eventually forms a stalk-like stem that pushes into the ground, swells, and grows into a peanut.

Walnuts are one of the most popular nuts used for baking; they provide texture, taste, and nutrition without overwhelming the flavor of the baked good, as is often the case with peanuts and other nuts. Walnuts have earned the nickname "brain food" for the wrinkled, brain-like appearance of their shell as well as their nutritional value. Though admittedly a high-fat food, walnuts are a good source of high-quality protein, vitamin E, calcium, iron, and zinc.

Honey Nut Crunch Bread

For a tasty alternative, try hazelnuts instead of walnuts.

1-pound loaf (8 – 10 servings):

1 cup water
2 1/2 teaspoons canola oil
1 1/2 tablespoons honey
1 teaspoon salt
3/4 cup oats
1 cup (5.4 ounces) whole wheat flour
3/4 cup (3.9 ounces) unbleached flour
1 1/2 tablespoons gluten flour
1/3 cup walnuts, chopped
3 tablespoons powdered whey
1 1/2 teaspoons active dry yeast

1 1/2-pound loaf (12 – 14 servings):

1 1/4 cups water
1 tablespoon canola oil
2 tablespoons honey
1 1/2 teaspoons salt
1 cup oats
1 1/2 cups (8.1 ounces) whole wheat flour
1 cup (5.2 ounces) unbleached flour
2 tablespoons gluten flour
1/2 cup walnuts, chopped
1/4 cup powdered whey
2 teaspoons active dry yeast

Put the ingredients in the bread pan in the order listed. Reverse the order if the manual for your machine calls for dry ingredients first. Select Basic Wheat Cycle, Light Setting (or the equivalent setting for your machine). Press Start.

Nutrient Analysis per Serving:
Calories: 178
Carbohydrates: 28
Protein: 7
Fat: 5
Fiber: 4

Sesame Seeds

Sesame appears to be the oldest crop grown for edible oil, and its seeds the earliest known condiment. Sesame seeds have long been valued for their nutritional riches; the command that opens the cave of treasure in the Arabian Nights' story of "Aladdin's Lamp" is "Open Sesame." The Egyptians used sesame seeds to make flour. Romans ground them into a paste used as a spread. Some of the best known Eastern dishes —hummus, tahini, and halvah — are made with ground sesame seeds.

Nutritionally, sesame seeds contain over 35 percent protein and are loaded with calcium. They are also rich in phosphorus, niacin, thiamin, and iron. Sesame oil is a natural salad oil and is unique because it requires little or no refining. Interestingly, the simple blend of 1 part soy to 1 part sesame has about the same nutritive value as the main protein in milk.

Sesame Seed Bread

Toasted sesame seeds lend a distinctively delicious flavor to this bread.

1-pound loaf (8 – 10 servings):
3/4 cup water
2 teaspoons canola oil
1 1/2 tablespoons honey
3/4 teaspoon salt
1 tablespoon toasted sesame seeds
1 1/4 cups (6.8 ounces) whole wheat flour
1/2 cup (2.6 ounces) unbleached flour
2 tablespoons gluten flour
1 1/2 tablespoons powdered whey
1 1/2 teaspoons active dry yeast

1 1/2-pound loaf (12 – 14 servings):
1 1/4 cups water
1 tablespoon canola oil
2 tablespoons honey
1 1/4 teaspoons salt
1 1/2 tablespoons toasted sesame seeds
2 1/4 cups (12.2 ounces) whole wheat flour
1/2 cup (2.6 ounces) unbleached flour
3 tablespoons gluten flour
2 tablespoons powdered whey
2 teaspoons active dry yeast

Put the ingredients in the bread pan in the order listed, or in the reverse order if the manual for your machine calls for dry ingredients first and liquids last. Select Basic Wheat Cycle, Light Setting (or the equivalent setting for your machine). Push Start.

Nutrient Analysis per Serving:
Calories: 128
Carbohydrates: 24
Protein: 5
Fat: 2
Fiber: 3

Flax and Flaxseed

Flax is a herbaceous annual that originated in prehistoric times in the Mediterranean. Flaxseeds and flaxseed oil are best known for being a rich source of protein and of omega-3 essential fatty acids (EFAs). Omega-3s have an astounding range of beneficial health effects, including the ability to lower high blood cholesterol and triglyceride levels, inhibit tumor formation, aid in preventing heart disease, and help those with arthritis, diabetes, allergies, asthma, PMS, and inflammatory skin conditions such as eczema. Flaxseeds are a popular nutritional supplement because our diets commonly lack adequate amounts of the EFAs. In the U.S., the most common dietary source is fatty, coldwater fish, such as salmon, which contains only half as much EFAs as flaxseed oil. The hormone-like compounds in flaxseed, known as lignans, are currently being investigated as anticancer agents, especially for estrogen-dependent cancers like some breast cancer. Although other seeds, grains, and legumes also contain lignans, flaxseeds are the richest plant source.

Flaxseed Bread

A delicious source of protein.

1-pound loaf (8 – 10 servings):

3/4 cup water
1 tablespoon olive oil
2 teaspoons Sucanat™
1 teaspoon salt
1/3 cup flaxseed
1 1/3 cup (7.2 ounces) whole wheat flour
1/3 cup (1.7 ounces) unbleached flour
1 1/2 tablespoon gluten flour
1 tablespoon powdered whey
1 1/2 teaspoons active dry yeast

1 1/2-pound loaf (12 – 14 servings):

1 cup plus 2 tablespoons water
1 1/2 tablespoons olive oil
1 tablespoon Sucanat™
1 teaspoon salt
1/2 cup flaxseed
2 cups (10.8 ounces) whole wheat flour
1/2 cup (2.6 ounces) unbleached flour
2 tablespoons gluten flour
1 1/2 tablespoons powdered whey
1 1/2 teaspoons active dry yeast

Put the ingredients in the bread pan in the order listed, or in the reverse order if the manual for your machine calls for dry ingredients first and liquids last. Select Basic Wheat Cycle, Light Setting (or the equivalent setting for your machine). Push Start.

Nutrient Analysis per Serving:
Calories: 119
Carbohydrates: 19
Protein: 5
Fat: 3
Fiber: 4

Poppy Seeds

Many kinds of poppy flowers are grown for ornament, but only the seeds of the opium poppy have culinary importance. A native of the Middle East, opium was used as a medicine by the Egyptians, Greeks, and Romans. Opium is made from the gummy latex contained in green, unripe poppy seeds. This latex oozes out when the seeds are slit open. Opium contains over 24 different alkaloids with known medicinal and narcotic effects. The ripe seed, which is used in cooking, contains no alkaloids and can therefore be used whole, pressed, or ground for sheer gustatory pleasure.

Two types of poppy seeds are used in cooking. The most common type is blue-grey shot, widely used here and in Europe in baked goods or as a topping for yeast breads. The other type of poppy seed differs little in flavor but is smaller, with a creamy yellow color. It is commonly used in India both to flavor curries and to thicken and improve the texture of sauces.

Perfect Poppy Seed Bread

Light and lemony, a perfect teatime bread!

1-pound loaf (8 – 10 servings):

- 3/4 cup plus 1 tablespoon water
- 1 tablespoon canola oil
- 1 teaspoon salt
- 1 cup (5.4 ounces) whole wheat flour
- 1 cup (5.2 ounces) unbleached flour
- 1 1/2 tablespoons gluten flour
- 2 teaspoons lemon peel, grated
- 2 tablespoons poppy seeds
- 1 tablespoon powdered whey
- 2 teaspoons active dry yeast

1 1/2-pound loaf (12 – 14 servings):

- 1 1/4 cups water
- 1 1/2 tablespoons canola oil
- 1 1/2 teaspoons salt
- 1 1/2 cups (8.1 ounces) whole wheat flour
- 1 1/2 cups (7.8 ounces) unbleached flour
- 2 tablespoons gluten flour
- 1 tablespoon lemon peel, grated
- 3 tablespoons poppy seeds
- 1 1/2 tablespoons powdered whey
- 2 1/2 teaspoons active dry yeast

RECIPE TIP

Use organic lemon, or wash with a cleanser formulated to remove pesticides, such as Trillium Health Products™ Nature's Wash®.

Put the ingredients in the bread pan in the order listed, or in the reverse order if the manual for your machine calls for dry ingredients first and liquids last. Select Basic Wheat Cycle, Light Setting (or the equivalent setting for your machine). Push Start.

Nutrient Analysis per Serving:
Calories: 106
Carbohydrates: 23
Protein: 5
Fat: 1
Fiber: 3

Protein Complementation

Protein complementation is poorly understood by most people, particularly in America, where the perceived need for protein reaches obsessive levels. It is true that we need proteins to build and repair our body and to sustain life, but obtaining sufficient protein is easier than you think. The reason is that there are 22 amino acids. Of the 22, our bodies can make all but 9 in sufficient amounts. These remaining 9 are called essential amino acids and must be supplied by the diet. Almost all animal foods are good sources of protein. Plant foods are not considered good sources of "complete" protein because they are frequently low in 1 or 2 of the 9 acids. However, by consuming plant foods with "complementary" amino acid content, it is easy to enjoy a high-quality protein meal without relying on animal products. For example, eat corn, which is low in lysine but high in methionine, and beans, which are low in methionine but high in lysine. What's more, complementary plant foods don't need to be eaten at the same meal, just within the same day.

Multi-Seed Bread

A savory aromatic bread with bites of extra flavor spread throughout.

1-pound loaf (8 – 10 servings):

3/4 cup water
1 tablespoon canola oil
1 1/2 tablespoons honey
1/2 teaspoon salt
1/4 teaspoon poppy seeds
1/2 teaspoon celery seeds
1 cup (5.4 ounces) whole wheat flour
1 cup (5.2 ounces) unbleached flour
1 1/2 teaspoons active dry yeast

1 1/2-pound loaf (12 – 14 servings):

1 1/4 cups water
1 1/2 tablespoons canola oil
2 tablespoons honey
1 teaspoon salt
1/2 teaspoon poppy seeds
3/4 teaspoon celery seeds
1 1/2 cups (8.1 ounces) whole wheat flour
1 1/2 cups (7.8 ounces) unbleached flour
2 teaspoons active dry yeast

Put the ingredients in the bread pan in the order listed, or in the reverse order if the manual for your machine calls for dry ingredients first and liquids last. Select Basic Wheat Cycle, Light Setting (or the equivalent setting for your machine). Push Start.

Nutrient Analysis per Serving:
Calories: 122
Carbohydrates: 23
Protein: 4
Fat: 2
Fiber: 2

Seeds

Like nuts, seeds are a nutritionally superior food supplying generous amounts of many vitamins, minerals, and protein, which makes them a good substitute for animal protein. Seeds, unfortunately, are also about 50 percent fat by weight, so they're best eaten in moderation. But, unlike most animal sources of protein, which are rich in artery-clogging saturated fat and cholesterol, the fats in seeds are largely polyunsaturated and monounsaturated and are gentler on the circulatory system. In addition, like all plant foods, seeds do not contain cholesterol. Some commonly used seeds include sunflower, sesame, poppy, caraway, flax, and pumpkin.

Adding sunflower seeds is a great way to fortify breads. In addition to their protein content, sunflower seeds are a rich source of linoleic acid, an essential fatty acid. Sunflower seeds are also a good source of vitamin E, the B vitamins, and many minerals, including iron. In fact, a serving of sunflower seeds contains over 30 percent more iron than a serving of raisins, a popular source of iron.

Sunflower Seed Bread

The distinct flavor of sunflower seeds makes this a favorite for kids of any age.

1-pound loaf (8 – 10 servings):
3/4 cup plus 1 tablespoon water
3/4 tablespoon canola oil
1 1/2 tablespoons honey
1/2 teaspoon salt
2 teaspoons gluten flour
1 1/2 cups (8.1 ounces) whole wheat flour
1/2 cup (2.6 ounces) unbleached flour
1/4 cup sunflower kernels
1 1/2 teaspoons active dry yeast

1 1/2-pound loaf (12 – 14 servings):
1 1/4 cups water
1 tablespoon canola oil
2 tablespoons honey
3/4 teaspoon salt
1 tablespoon gluten flour
2 1/4 cups (12.2 ounces) whole wheat flour
3/4 cup (3.9 ounces) unbleached flour
1/3 cup sunflower kernels
2 teaspoons active dry yeast

Put the ingredients in the bread pan in the order listed, or in the reverse order if the manual for your machine calls for dry ingredients first and liquids last. Select Basic Wheat Cycle, Light Setting (or the equivalent setting for your machine). Push Start.

Nutrient Analysis per Serving:
Calories: 103
Carbohydrates: 17
Protein: 5
Fat: 3
Fiber: 3

Pineapple

Pineapples probably originated in Brazil and are native to South America. Explorers brought pineapples home to Europe, where the fruit was grown in hothouses in the 1700s. The pineapple quickly became a favorite fruit of rich Europeans. Pineapple plantations were established in tropical regions, and the fruit was produced in Florida from the 1860s to early 1900s.

Fresh pineapples are not only delicious, they also contain bromelain, a protein-digesting enzyme with anti-inflammatory properties. Tests show that bromelain can ease the pain and swelling associated with inflammatory conditions such as arthritis.

Hawaiian Nut Bread

*You'll feel like saying "Aloha!" when you treat your-
self to this tropical delight.*

1-pound loaf (8 – 10 servings):

3/4 cup plus 1 tablespoon water
1 1/2 teaspoons vegetable oil
2 tablespoons honey
2/3 teaspoon salt
1 1/3 cups (7.2 ounces) whole wheat flour
2/3 cup (3.5 ounces) unbleached white flour
2 tablespoons gluten flour
1/2 cup dehydrated pineapple, chopped
1/2 cup macadamia nuts, chopped
2 tablespoons powdered whey
1 1/2 teaspoons active dry yeast

1 1/2-pound loaf (12 – 14 servings):

1 1/3 cups water
1/2 tablespoon vegetable oil
3 tablespoons honey
1 teaspoon salt
2 cups (10.8 ounces) whole wheat flour
1 cup (5.2 ounces) unbleached white flour
3 tablespoons gluten flour
2/3 cup dehydrated pineapple, chopped
1 cup macadamia nuts, chopped
3 tablespoons powdered whey
2 teaspoons active dry yeast

Put the ingredients in the bread pan in the
order listed, or in the reverse order if the
manual for your machine calls for dry
ingredients first and liquids last. Select
Basic Wheat Cycle, Light Setting (or
the equivalent setting for your
machine). Push Start.

RECIPE TIP

*Try to find dried
fruits without
sulfites or
added sugar.*

Nutrient Analysis per Serving:
Calories: 179
Carbohydrates: 27
Protein: 5
Fat: 6
Fiber: 4

149

Almonds

The almond is thought to have originated in Western Asia and North Africa. Northern California is the area that grows the most almonds in the world; almonds grow best when summers are long and hot and winters are mild. Almond production is second only to that of grapes in California.

Almonds are packed full of nutrients. They are rich in polyunsaturated oils and are a good source of protein (12 percent), potassium, calcium, iron, zinc, and vitamin E. However, almonds should be used sparingly as a garnish due to their high fat content (80 percent). Half a cup of almonds contains over 400 calories.

Amazing Almond Amaranth Bread

Amaranth and almonds add the crunch that makes this chewy, dense bread a triple A treat!

1-pound loaf (8 – 10 servings):

3/4 cup plus 1 tablespoon water
1 tablespoon canola oil
1 1/3 tablespoons Sucanat™
3/4 teaspoon salt
1/2 cup rolled oats
1 1/3 tablespoons amaranth grain
1/3 cup amaranth flour
1 1/3 cups (7.2 ounces) whole wheat flour
2 tablespoons gluten flour
1/2 cup almonds, chopped
1 1/3 tablespoons powdered whey
1 1/2 teaspoons active dry yeast

1 1/2-pound loaf (12 – 14 servings):

1 1/3 cups water
1 1/2 tablespoons canola oil
2 tablespoons Sucanat™
1 teaspoon salt
2/3 cup rolled oats
2 tablespoons amaranth grain
1/2 cup amaranth flour
2 cups (10.8 ounces) whole wheat flour
3 tablespoons gluten flour
3/4 cup almonds, chopped
2 tablespoons powdered whey
2 teaspoons active dry yeast

Put the ingredients in the bread pan in the order listed, or in the reverse order if the manual for your machine calls for dry ingredients first and liquids last. Select Basic Wheat Cycle, Light Setting (or the equivalent setting for your machine). Push Start.

Nutrient Analysis per Serving:
Calories: 146
Carbohydrates: 20
Protein: 5.4
Fat: 5.7
Fiber: 3

Anise

Anise is an annual herb that has been cultivated for its strong licorice flavor and medicinal properties since the sixth century B.C. Hippocrates prescribed anise for coughs, and the Roman scholar Pliny believed that anise removed all bad odors from the mouth if chewed in the morning, a use still recommended today. Because of the value of anise, it was one of the spices used by the Romans to pay taxes. In the sixteenth century, anise was used as mousetrap bait, which, according to old herbals, mice found irresistible. Dogs love the scent of anise as well, and it is said that what catnip is to cats, anise is to dogs. In greyhound racing, the artificial hare is scented with anise.

Anise imparts a refined and consistent licorice flavor to foods and is complemented by cinnamon and bay. Anise leaves can also be used whole or dried to make teas.

Anise Bread

Anise adds a spicy, sweet licorice flavor yet isn't over-whelming. This Middle Eastern spice will delight your senses.

1-pound loaf (8 – 10 servings):

3/4 cup plus 1 tablespoon water
1 tablespoon canola oil
1 tablespoon honey
3/4 teaspoon salt
1 cup (5.4 ounces) whole wheat flour
1 cup (5.2 ounces) unbleached flour
2 teaspoons gluten flour
1 teaspoon anise seeds
1/8 teaspoon mace (optional)
1/8 teaspoon nutmeg
1/2 teaspoon lemon zest
1 1/2 tablespoons powdered whey
1 1/2 teaspoons active dry yeast

1 1/2-pound loaf (12 – 14 servings):

1 1/4 cups water
1 1/2 tablespoons canola oil
2 tablespoons honey
1 teaspoon salt
1 1/2 cups (8.1 ounces) whole wheat flour
1 1/2 cups (7.8 ounces) unbleached flour
1 tablespoon gluten flour
1 1/2 teaspoons anise seeds
1/8 teaspoon mace (optional)
1/8 teaspoon nutmeg
3/4 teaspoon lemon zest
2 tablespoons powdered whey
2 teaspoons active dry yeast

Put the ingredients in the bread pan in the order listed, or in the reverse order if the manual for your machine calls for dry ingredients first and liquids last. Select Basic Wheat Cycle, Light Setting (or the equivalent setting for your machine). Push Start.

Nutrient Analysis per Serving:
Calories: 124   *Fat: 2*
Carbohydrates: 23   *Fiber: 2*
Protein: 5

CHAPTER NINE

Herb Breads

Basil

Of the many species of basil, the most common is sweet basil (ocimum basilicum). This annual plant has green, leafy stems that give it a bushy appearance. Basil can grow to a height of 2 feet but is usually pruned lower. Native to India, Africa, and Asia, basil is now cultivated extensively throughout much of the world. In addition to basil's use as an aromatic herb, its aromatic oil is used in cordials, cosmetics, perfumes, and soaps. In China, the medicinal use of basil can be traced back over 3,000 years, and the herb is still used there to treat spasms of the intestinal tract, kidney ailments, and impaired circulation.

Fresh basil, which is the most aromatic, can often be found in grocery stores. Look for leaves of a crisp vibrant green with no browning or signs of decay. Though it can never replace the fresh herb in flavor, dried basil is one of the most widely used herbs for cooking. Basil is a natural with tomatoes and green beans and in stews, pasta sauces, and soups.

Basil Cheese Bread

This classic combination is a perfect accompaniment for all your Italian meals.

1-pound loaf (8 – 10 servings):

3/4 cup plus 1 tablespoon water
1 tablespoon canola oil
2 teaspoons honey
1/2 teaspoon salt
1/4 cup Parmesan cheese, grated
2 teaspoons dried basil
1 1/2 cups (8.1 ounces) whole wheat flour
1/2 cup (2.6 ounces) unbleached flour
1 1/3 tablespoons gluten flour
1 tablespoon powdered whey
1 1/2 teaspoons active dry yeast

1 1/2-pound loaf (12 – 14 servings):

1 1/4 cups water
1 1/2 tablespoons canola oil
1 tablespoon honey
1 teaspoon salt
1/3 cup Parmesan cheese, grated
1 tablespoon dried basil
2 1/4 cups (12.2 ounces) whole wheat flour
3/4 cup (3.9 ounces) unbleached white flour
2 tablespoons gluten flour
2 tablespoons powdered whey
2 teaspoons active dry yeast

Put the ingredients in the bread pan in the order listed, or in the reverse order if the manual for your machine calls for dry ingredients first and liquids last. Select Basic Wheat Cycle, Light Setting (or the equivalent setting for your machine). Push Start.

Nutrient Analysis per Serving:
Calories: 127
Carbohydrates: 21
Protein: 4
Fat: 2
Fiber: 2

Parsley

Parsley is extremely rich in chlorophyll, the green pigment of plants. Chlorophyll acts much like the hemoglobin in our bodies, transporting oxygen to the cells, and interestingly, is structurally identical to hemoglobin but with one important difference. In hemoglobin, the central oxygen-carrying molecule is iron, whereas in chlorophyll, it is magnesium. The high chlorophyll content of parsley is thought to be responsible for parsley's powerful anti-cancer effects; however, parsley has benefits well beyond its chlorophyll content. It has long been used for medicinal purposes and is regarded as an excellent nerve stimulant. Empirical evidence seems to support the claims of many juice enthusiasts who label parsley-containing juices "energy drinks." Parsley is a nutritional dynamo, rich in protein, calcium, iron, potassium, vitamin A, and vitamin C.

Long ago, the seeds of parsley were used as a condiment. Today, its leaves are usually used as a flavoring or garnish. The kind of parsley most Americans are familiar with is the one with the small, curly leaves. Another variety, currently sold in the produce sections of many stores, has much larger, flat leaves.

Parsley Parmesan Bread

A unique twist with a fresh taste, this is a loaf you'll bake often.

1-pound loaf (8 – 10 servings):
3/4 cup plus 1 tablespoon water
1 tablespoon canola oil
3 teaspoons honey
1/2 teaspoon salt
3 tablespoons Parmesan cheese, grated
1 1/2 teaspoons parsley
1/2 teaspoon chives
1 teaspoon dried basil
1 1/3 cups (7.2 ounces) whole wheat flour
1/2 cup (2.6 ounces) unbleached flour
1 1/2 tablespoons gluten flour
1 tablespoon powdered whey
1 1/2 teaspoons active dry yeast

1 1/2-pound loaf (12 – 14 servings):
1 1/4 cups water
1 1/2 tablespoons canola oil
1 tablespoon honey
1 teaspoon salt
1/4 cup Parmesan cheese, grated
2 teaspoons parsley
2/3 teaspoon chives
1 1/3 teaspoons dried basil
2 cups (10.8 ounces) whole wheat flour
3/4 cup (3.9 ounces) unbleached flour
2 tablespoons gluten flour
1 1/3 tablespoons powdered whey
2 teaspoons active dry yeast

Put the ingredients in the bread pan in the order listed, or in the reverse order if the manual for your machine calls for dry ingredients first and liquids last. Select Basic Wheat Cycle, Light Setting (or the equivalent setting for your machine). Push Start.

Nutrient Analysis per Serving:
Calories: 127   *Fat: 2*
Carbohydrates: 21   *Fiber: 2*
Protein: 4

Kitchen Herb Boxes

Have you ever started a recipe only to find that it calls for the addition of a small amount of a fresh herb that you don't have?

You can prevent this inconvenience and save money by growing your own! To make your own, all you need is either a collection of small pots or a large, shallow potting container. Add potting soil and your favorite herb seeds, place the container in a sunny spot, and water the herbs every 2 days. After the plants start to grow, they can either be snipped and used fresh, chopped and frozen for later use, or transplanted to a garden plot outdoors. Either way, they're easy to make and enjoyable to look at and care for, and add a sweet, authentic fragrance to your home.

Classic Herb Bread

Full of character, this bread adds a special flair to any meal.

1-pound loaf (8 – 10 servings):

3/4 cup water
1 tablespoon olive oil
1 teaspoon honey
1/2 teaspoon salt
1/3 teaspoon oregano
1/3 teaspoon thyme
1/3 teaspoon pepper
1/8 teaspoon celery seed
2 1/2 tablespoons wheat germ
1 2/3 cups (9 ounces) whole wheat flour
2 tablespoons gluten flour
2 tablespoons powdered whey
1 1/2 teaspoons active dry yeast

1 1/2-pound loaf (12 – 14 servings):

1 1/8 cups water
1 1/2 tablespoons olive oil
1 1/2 teaspoons honey
1 1/3 teaspoons salt
1/2 teaspoon oregano
1/2 teaspoon thyme
1/2 teaspoon pepper
1/4 teaspoon celery seed
1/4 cup wheat germ
2 1/2 cups (13.5 ounces) whole wheat flour
3 tablespoons gluten flour
3 tablespoons powdered whey
2 teaspoons active dry yeast

Put the ingredients in the bread pan in the order listed, or in the reverse order if the manual for your machine calls for dry ingredients first and liquids last. Select Basic Wheat Cycle, Light Setting (or the equivalent setting for your machine). Push Start.

Nutrient Analysis per Serving:

Calories: 115	*Fat: 2*
Carbohydrates: 19	*Fiber: 3*
Protein: 5	

161

Chives

The chive differs from most of its relatives in the onion (allium genus) family of vegetables in that the leaves, not the bulb, are the edible portion of the plant. Known for their mild flavor, chives add a delightful accent to salads, dips, casseroles, omelets, sauces, and spreads. Chives are sold dried as a spice or fresh in the vegetable section. Fresh chives keep only a few days in the refrigerator, but the leaves can be chopped and stored in a plastic bag in the freezer.

Chives are one of the easiest vegetables to grow. Many cooks keep chives in their kitchen in a small pot and just snip off leaves as needed. Besides adding an appetizing flavor to many recipes, chives are also a good source of iron, potassium, and vitamin C and an excellent source of vitamin A.

Garden-Fresh Herb Bread

There's nothing like the flavor of fresh summer herbs to add a special touch to your favorite recipes. Experiment and enjoy.

1-pound loaf (8 – 10 servings):

3/4 cup plus 1 tablespoon water
2 tablespoons olive oil
1/2 teaspoon honey
1 teaspoon salt
1/4 teaspoon dried chives
1/2 teaspoon tarragon
1 cup (5.4 ounces) whole wheat flour
1 cup (5.2 ounces) unbleached flour
2 tablespoons gluten flour
2 tablespoons powdered whey
1 1/2 teaspoons active dry yeast

1 1/2-pound loaf (12 – 14 servings):

1 1/4 cups water
3 tablespoons olive oil
1 teaspoon honey
1 1/2 teaspoons salt
1/3 teaspoon dried chives
3/4 teaspoon tarragon
1 1/2 cups (8.1 ounces) whole wheat flour
1 1/2 cups (7.8 ounces) unbleached flour
3 1/2 tablespoons gluten flour
3 1/2 tablespoons powdered whey
2 teaspoons active dry yeast

Put the ingredients in the bread pan in the order listed, or in the reverse order if the manual for your machine calls for dry ingredients first and liquids last. Select Basic Wheat Cycle, Light Setting (or the equivalent setting for your machine). Push Start.

Nutrient Analysis per Serving:
Calories: 138
Carbohydrates: 23
Protein: 5
Fat: 3
Fiber: 2

163

Olives

In countries bordering the Mediterranean, olives are nearly a staple food. Fresh olives are put in a saltwater bath that is changed on a daily basis. The olives are kept in this bath until they are soft, dark, and ready for eating. Olives packed in jars with brine can be safely stored without sodium benzoate, a commonly added preservative.

The word brine refers to a saltwater solution, so even if salt is not listed on the label, it's in the jar. Next to fresh olives, brine-packed olives are the most flavorful. Three types of olives are available: ripe green olives, ripe black olives, and tree-ripened or home-cured olives. Black olives are dipped in ferrous gluconate, a completely harmless salt, to color them. Though olives add a delicious taste to many types of salads and entrees, keep in mind that with a 93 percent fat content, olives are rich in calories as well as sodium and are best used sparingly by those following heart-healthy diets.

Mediterranean Bread

Try it with a mixed green salad and cioppino.

1-pound loaf (8 – 10 servings):

3/4 cup water
2 teaspoons olive oil
1 tablespoon honey
2 tablespoons feta cheese, crumbled
4 teaspoons black olives, chopped
2 1/2 tablespoons cucumber, peeled, seeded, and pureed
1 teaspoon salt
1 1/2 cups (8.1 ounces) whole wheat flour
2/3 cup (3.5 ounces) unbleached flour
1 tablespoon gluten flour
1/8 teaspoon garlic powder
1/2 teaspoon thyme
1/2 teaspoon dill
2 teaspoons powdered whey
1 1/2 teaspoons active dry yeast

1 1/2-pound loaf (12 – 14 servings):

1 1/4 cups water
1 tablespoon olive oil
1 1/2 tablespoons honey
1/4 cup feta cheese, crumbled
2 tablespoons black olives, chopped
1/4 cup cucumber, peeled, seeded, and pureed
1 1/2 teaspoons salt
2 cups (10.8 ounces) whole wheat flour
1 cup (5.2 ounces) unbleached flour
1 1/2 tablespoons gluten flour
1/4 teaspoon garlic powder
3/4 teaspoon thyme
3/4 teaspoon dill
1 tablespoon powdered whey
2 teaspoons active dry yeast

Follow the instructions for other breads in this chapter.

Nutrient Analysis per Serving:
Calories: 127
Carbohydrates: 22
Protein: 5

Fat: 2
Fiber: 3

Sweet Marjoram

Sweet marjoram is a subtly perfumed, calming herb widely used in a variety of dishes. The mild flavor of marjoram resembles oregano and is complemented by bay, garlic, onion, thyme, and basil.

The Greeks called the marjoram plant "joy of the mountains." Young Greek couples were crowned with it at weddings. Marjoram has mild antioxidant and antifungal properties, and marjoram gargles and teas might help relieve sinus congestion and hay fever. As an aromatic, marjoram is also used to help scent chests and linen closets. Marjoram is a popular addition to baths for its aromatic, soothing scent and mild antiseptic qualities, which benefit the skin.

Savory Herb Bread

This makes a mean veggie sandwich.

1-pound loaf (8 – 10 servings)

- 3/4 cup plus 1 tablespoon water
- 1 tablespoon canola oil
- 1 tablespoon honey
- 1 teaspoon salt
- 1 1/2 cups (8.1 ounces) whole wheat flour
- 2/3 cup (3.5 ounces) unbleached flour
- 2 tablespoons gluten flour
- 1 teaspoon chives
- 1 teaspoon marjoram
- 1 teaspoon thyme
- 1/2 teaspoon basil
- 1 tablespoon powdered whey
- 1 1/2 teaspoons active dry yeast

1 1/2-pound loaf (12 – 14 servings):

- 1 1/4 cups water
- 1 1/2 tablespoons canola oil
- 2 tablespoons honey
- 1 1/2 teaspoons salt
- 2 cups (10.8 ounces) whole wheat flour
- 1 cup (5.2 ounces) unbleached flour
- 3 tablespoons gluten flour
- 1/2 tablespoon chives
- 1/2 tablespoon marjoram
- 1/2 tablespoon thyme
- 1 teaspoon basil
- 1 1/2 tablespoons powdered whey
- 2 teaspoons active dry yeast

Put the ingredients in the bread pan in the order listed, or in the reverse order if the manual for your machine calls for dry ingredients first and liquids last. Select Basic Wheat Cycle, Light Setting (or the equivalent setting for your machine). Push Start.

RECIPE TIP

This recipe is intended for dried flaked herbs. If you use ground herbs, reduce the amount by half. If you use fresh herbs, use twice as much.

Nutrient Analysis per Serving:

Calories: 127	Fat: 2
Carbohydrates: 23	Fiber: 2
Protein: 5	

Garlic

Garlic is a member of the lily family and is cultivated worldwide. The garlic bulb is composed of individual cloves enclosed in a white skin. Throughout recorded history, beginning 5,000 years ago in Sanskirt records in India, the lowly garlic bulb has been acclaimed as a potent medical remedy for a wide variety of conditions. The Chinese have used garlic for 3,000 years, and the Egyptians since at least 1550 B.C. In the West, we have applied garlic to medical problems since the time of Hippocrates, and modern scientists have now discovered its secrets. The reason garlic can lower cholesterol; prevent blood clots; treat viral, bacterial, fungal, yeast, and tubercular infections; inhibit tumors; detoxify the body of lead and mercury; and reduce the need for insulin in diabetics is organic sulfur compounds that include allicin, the compound that gives the bulb its distinctive scent. Consumers looking for some of garlic's medical benefits without its aroma can buy deodorized capsules in health food stores. Be forewarned, however, that for its antibiotic, antifungal properties, the odoriferous allicin is needed. In cooking, garlic complements grains and vegetables and tastes delicious both in and on fresh-baked bread.

Garlic Bread

A must with spaghetti and lasagna!

1 pound loaf (8-10 servings):

3/4 cup plus 1 tablespoon water
1/2 tablespoon canola oil
1 tablespoon honey
1/4 cup Parmesan cheese, grated
1/2 teaspoon minced fresh garlic
1 teaspoon salt
1 1/2 cups (8.1 ounces) whole wheat flour
2/3 cup (3.5 ounces) unbleached flour
1/2 teaspoon sweet basil
1/4 teaspoon garlic powder
1 1/2 teaspoons active dry yeast

1 1/2-pound loaf (12-14 servings):

1 1/4 cups water
3/4 tablespoon canola oil
1 1/2 tablespoons honey
1/3 cup Parmesan cheese, grated
3/4 teaspoon minced fresh garlic
1 1/2 teaspoons salt
2 cups (10.8 ounces) whole wheat flour
1 cup (5.2 ounces) unbleached flour
3/4 teaspoon sweet basil
1/2 teaspoon garlic powder
2 teaspoons active dry yeast

RECIPE TIP

For the most flavorful result, grate your own Parmesan cheese. Also, be sure to check the consistency of the dough.

Put the ingredients in the bread pan in the order listed, or in the reverse order if the manual for your machine calls for dry ingredients first and liquids last. Select Basic Wheat Cycle, Light Setting (or the equivalent setting for your machine). Push Start.

Nutrient Analysis per Serving:
Calories: 120
Carbohydrates: 22
Protein: 5

Fat: 2
Fiber: 3

Black Pepper

Black pepper is one of the most widely used seasoning agents in the U.S. and accounts for $1/4$ of the world's total spice production. Many people consider pepper an irritant detrimental to health. However, pepper has actually been used as a medicine for thousands of years. Black pepper contains the alkaloid piperine, which is a stimulant. It improves digestion by stimulating the taste buds, causing an increase in stomach acid secretion. Pepper also has impressive antibacterial properties. Because the characteristic flavor of pepper diminishes when exposed to air, freshly ground pepper is always preferred.

Black Pepper Bread

You'll love this moist, spicy bread — a real gourmet sandwich bread.

1-pound loaf (8 – 10 servings):
1/2 cup water
2 teaspoons canola oil
1 tablespoon honey
2/3 cup firm tofu
3/4 teaspoon salt
1 cup (5.4 ounces) whole wheat flour
3/4 cup (3.9 ounces) unbleached flour
1/2 teaspoon black pepper
3/4 teaspoon chives
1 1/2 teaspoons active dry yeast

1 1/2-pound loaf (12 – 14 servings):
3/4 cup water
1 tablespoon canola oil
1 1/2 tablespoons honey
1 cup firm tofu
1 teaspoon salt
1 1/2 cups (8.1 ounces) whole wheat flour
1 cup (5.2 ounces) unbleached flour
2/3 teaspoon black pepper
1 teaspoon chives
2 teaspoons active dry yeast

Put the ingredients in the bread pan in the order listed, or in the reverse order if the manual for your machine calls for dry ingredients first and liquids last. Select Basic Wheat Cycle, Light Setting (or the equivalent setting for your machine). Push Start.

Nutrient Analysis per Serving:
Calories: 121
Carbohydrates: 19
Protein: 6
Fat: 3
Fiber: 2

RECIPE TIP

Do not use the timer cycle for this bread. Tofu is highly perishable.

Soy Cheese

Soy cheese is comparable to cheese made from cow's milk in calories, protein, fat, and sodium content. However, soy cheese is cholesterol-free and lactose-free and low in saturated fat. Soy cheese, which tastes and cooks somewhat like its dairy counterpart, is a boon to those who are lactose intolerant or who have been advised to restrict the amount of saturated fat and cholesterol in their diet. Soy cheese is made with vegetable gums and also contains either the milk derivative calcium caseinate (which means it is not strictly dairy-free) or isolated soy protein. Although not as widely available as regular cheese, soy cheese has been growing in popularity and can be found in natural food stores.

Garlic Herb Cheese Bread

This delightful trio of ingredients makes a perfect picnic bread.

1-pound loaf (8 – 10 servings):
3/4 cup water
2 teaspoons canola oil
1 1/2 tablespoons honey
1/2 teaspoon salt
1 1/8 cups (6.1 ounces) whole wheat flour
2/3 cup (3.5 ounces) unbleached flour
2 teaspoons gluten flour
1/3 cup soy cheese, grated
1 1/2 teaspoons basil
1 teaspoon garlic powder
2/3 teaspoon thyme
1 tablespoon powdered whey
1 1/2 teaspoons active dry yeast

1 1/2-pound loaf (12 – 14 servings):
1 1/8 cups water
1 tablespoon canola oil
2 tablespoons honey
1 teaspoon salt
1 3/4 cups (9.5 ounces) whole wheat flour
1 cup (5.2 ounces) unbleached flour
1 tablespoon gluten flour
1/2 cup soy cheese, grated
2 teaspoons basil
2 teaspoons garlic powder
1 teaspoon thyme
2 tablespoons powdered whey
2 teaspoons active dry yeast

Put the ingredients in the bread pan in the order listed, or in the reverse order if the manual for your machine calls for dry ingredients first and liquids last. Select Basic Wheat Cycle, Light Setting (or the equivalent setting for your machine). Push Start.

Nutrient Analysis per Serving:
Calories: 144   *Fat: 3*
Carbohydrates: 23   *Fiber: 3*
Protein: 6

173

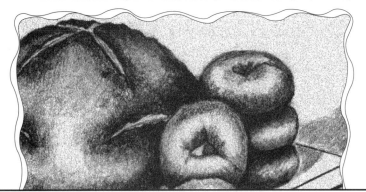

CHAPTER TEN

Handformed Breads

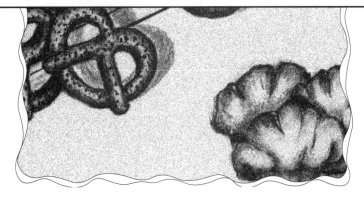

Bagels

Although they are now popular nationwide, bagels, an ethnic bread, used to be available only in metropolitan areas in the Northeast. The basic bagel recipe uses high-gluten flour, water, yeast, salt, oil, and sometimes malt. These essential ingredients can be varied by the addition of onion, caraway seed, sesame seed, poppy seed, raisins, sugar, and a small amount of whole wheat or rye flour. Some exceptional brands base their entire recipe on whole wheat and/or rye, but these are not readily available and can usually only be found in select bagel eateries or natural food stores.

Whole Wheat Bagels

Hearty, healthful bagels are a great way to begin the day.

1 pound loaf (8 – 10 servings):

3/4 cup plus 1 tablespoon water
2 1/2 teaspoons canola oil
1 tablespoon honey
1 teaspoon salt
1 1/3 cups (7.2 ounces) whole wheat flour
2/3 cup (3.5 ounces) unbleached flour
1 1/2 teaspoon active dry yeast

1 1/2-pound loaf (12 – 14 servings):

1 1/4 cups water
1 tablespoon canola oil
1 1/2 tablespoons honey
1 1/2 teaspoons salt
2 cups (10.8 ounces) whole wheat flour
1 cup (5.2 ounces) unbleached flour
2 teaspoons active dry yeast

1. Put the ingredients in the bread pan in the order listed, or in the reverse order if the manual for your machine calls for dry ingredients first and liquids last. Select the Dough cycle and press Start.

2. When the cycle is completed, take the dough out of the bread pan and cut into 8 or 12 portions (8 for 1-pound recipe, 12 for 1 1/2-pound recipe). Roll each portion into a smooth ball and then make a hole in the center with your fingers. The dough should resemble a doughnut.

3. Place bagels on a baking pan lined with wax paper. Cover them with a damp cloth. Let rise in a warm, draft-free place 30 to 40 minutes or until doubled in size.

4. Dip each ring into boiling water for 2 minutes and place on a lightly oiled baking pan.

5. Bake for 20 minutes at 400°F.

Nutrient Analysis per Serving: 1 bagel
Calories: 129   *Fat: 2*
Carbohydrates: 26   *Fiber: 3*
Protein: 4

Pizza

Pizza is without a doubt America's favorite take-out food. The beauty of making your own pizza, including the dough, is that you control all of the ingredients that go into it and can add as many fresh, healthy toppings as you want. Delicious whole grain vegetarian pizzas can be created by utilizing all of those "hidden" vegetables in your refrigerator. Experiment—you're certain to achieve a scrumptious product, better than any sold in the supermarket.

Cheese used to be considered a characteristic ingredient of pizza, but now that awareness of the health benefits of reducing fat intake is becoming widespread, most pizza shops will gladly serve a delicious pizza with all the trimmings—except the cheese.

Pizza Crust

There is nothing like freshly made pizza crust! You'll impress everyone with this easy and delicious recipe!

1-pound loaf (8 – 10 servings):
3/4 cup water
1 tablespoon canola oil
1 tablespoon honey
1 teaspoon salt
3/4 cup (4.1 ounces) whole wheat flour
1 cup (5.2 ounces) unbleached flour
1 1/2 teaspoons active dry yeast

1 1/2-pound loaf (12 – 14 servings):
1 1/4 cups water
1 1/2 tablespoons canola oil
1 1/2 tablespoons honey
1 1/2 teaspoons salt
1 1/4 cups (6.8 ounces) whole wheat flour
1 3/4 cups (9.1 ounces) unbleached flour
2 teaspoons active dry yeast

1. Put the ingredients in the bread pan in the order listed, or in the reverse order if the manual for your machine calls for dry ingredients first and liquids last. Select Dough Cycle. Press Start.

2. When the cycle is complete, remove the dough from the pan and place it in a lightly oiled bowl. Cover it with plastic wrap and let the dough sit in a warm, draft-free place for 20 to 30 minutes.

3. Remove dough from bowl and divide it into 2 portions, shaping each into a round ball. Cover with a clean cloth and let rest for about 15 minutes.

4. Roll out the dough into a circle and place on a lightly oiled pizza pan. Cover with your favorite pizza sauce and toppings and bake for 15 to 20 minutes at 400°F.

Nutrient Analysis per Serving: 1 slice
Calories: 165   *Fat: 2*
Carbohydrates: 31   *Fiber: 3*
Protein: 5

Pita Bread

Pita bread, or pocket bread, refers to a round bread that forms a pocket when cut crosswise. Once exclusively an ethnic bakery product, whole wheat pita is becoming more easily available. When prepared with whole wheat flour, water, yeast, salt, and occasionally vinegar but with no added sweeteners, fats, or chemicals, pita becomes a versatile and healthful alternative to bread for children's school lunches; it makes a sandwich with ingredients that won't drop out! Fill your pita with chopped vegetables, legumes, hummus, or a bean paté.

Pita Bread

So easy to make. Perfect for pocket sandwiches!

1-pound loaf (8 – 10 servings):
   3/4 cup water
   1 tablespoon canola oil
   1 tablespoon honey
   1 teaspoon salt
   1 1/2 cups (8.1 ounces) whole wheat flour
   1/2 cup (2.6 ounces) unbleached flour
   1 1/2 teaspoons active dry yeast

1 1/2-pound loaf (12 – 14 servings):
   1 1/4 cups water
   1 1/2 tablespoons canola oil
   1 1/2 tablespoons honey
   1 1/2 teaspoons salt
   2 1/8 cups (11.5 ounces) whole wheat flour
   3/4 cup (3.9 ounces) unbleached flour
   2 teaspoons active dry yeast

1. Put the ingredients in the bread pan in the order listed, or in the reverse order if the manual for your machine calls for dry ingredients first and liquids last. Select the Dough Cycle. Press Start.

2. When the cycle is completed, take the dough out of the bread pan and divide into 6 (1-pound recipe) or 8 (1 1/2 - pound recipe) pieces.

3. Roll each piece into a ball and let rise 20 to 30 minutes in a warm, draft-free place.

4. Flatten each ball into a disk about 5 to 6 inches in diameter. Place each disk on a baking sheet and bake at 500°F. for 8 to 10 minutes.

Nutrient Analysis per Serving: 1 pita
Calories: 190
Carbohydrates: 38
Protein: 7
Fat: 3
Fiber: 5

Bread Sticks

Whole wheat bread sticks are a delightful addition to any meal but go especially well with soup and salad. Salted or unsalted, they make a handy snack or appetizer. For an instant hit at your next party, try serving your whole wheat bread sticks with a spoonful of nut butter or a healthful spread or dip.

Bread Sticks

An excellent accompaniment to any Italian meal! You'll want to keep these healthful treats on hand for all occasions.

1-pound loaf (8 – 10 servings):

$^3/_4$ cup water
1 tablespoon canola oil
1 tablespoon honey
1 teaspoon salt
$^3/_4$ cup (4.1 ounces) whole wheat flour
1 cup (5.2 ounces) unbleached flour
1 $^1/_2$ teaspoons active dry yeast

1 $^1/_2$-pound loaf (12 – 14 servings):

1 $^1/_4$ cups water
1 $^1/_2$ tablespoons canola oil
1 $^1/_2$ tablespoons honey
1 $^1/_2$ teaspoons salt
1 $^1/_4$ cups (6.8 ounces) whole wheat flour
1 $^1/_2$ cups (7.8 ounces) unbleached flour
2 teaspoons active dry yeast

1. Put the ingredients in the bread pan in the order listed, or in the reverse order if the manual for your machine calls for dry ingredients first and liquids last. Select the Dough Cycle. Press Start.

2. When the cycle is completed, take dough out of the bread pan and cut into 14 to 16 pieces. Twist each piece into a rope, place onto a baking sheet and let rise in a warm, draft-free place for approximately 20 minutes. Sprinkle each with sesame seeds, poppy seeds, or other desired topping. Bake at 400°F for 15 minutes until golden brown.

Nutrient Analysis per Serving: 1 bread stick
Calories: 103
Carbohydrates: 19
Protein: 3
Fat: 2
Fiber: 2

Whole Wheat Pretzels

Wholesome and nutritious, the perfect snack.

1-pound loaf (8 – 10 servings)
3/4 cup water
1 tablespoon canola oil
1 tablespoon honey
1 teaspoon salt
1 3/4 cups (9.5 ounces) whole wheat flour
1 1/2 teaspoons active dry yeast

1 1/2-pound loaf (12 – 14 servings):
1 1/4 cups water
1 1/2 tablespoons canola oil
1 1/2 tablespoons honey
1 1/2 teaspoons salt
2 3/4 cups (14.9 ounces) whole wheat flour
2 teaspoons active dry yeast

1. Put the ingredients in the bread pan in the order listed, or in the reverse order if the manual for your machine calls for dry ingredients first and liquids last. Select the Dough Cycle. Press Start.

2. When the cycle is complete, remove the dough and cut into 10 (1-pound recipe) or 16 (1 1/2-pound recipe) strips.

3. Roll each strip into a rope and shape ropes into pretzels. (See diagram.) Cover and let rise in a warm, draft-free place for about 45 minutes.

4. Bring 2 quarts of water with 4 teaspoons baking soda to a boil, then turn down heat to maintain a light simmer. Gently place each pretzel in the water with a slotted spoon. It is easiest to do each pretzel separately. Leave pretzels in the water approximately 1 minute, turning once.

5. Remove the pretzels and place on a lightly oiled baking pan. Sprinkle with coarse salt, poppy seeds, or sesame seeds, if desired.

6. Bake at 475°F. for 12 minutes.

Nutrient Analysis per Serving: 1 pretzel
Calories: 95   *Fat: 2*
Carbohydrates: 18   *Fiber: 3*
Protein: 3

Light Wheat Pretzels

A tasty variation of whole wheat pretzels.

1-pound loaf (8 – 10 servings):

$3/4$ cup water

1 tablespoon canola oil

1 tablespoon honey

1 teaspoon salt

$3/4$ cup (4.1 ounces) whole wheat flour

1 cup (5.2 ounces) unbleached flour

1 $1/2$ teaspoons active dry yeast

1 $1/2$-pound loaf (12 – 14 servings):

1 $1/8$ cups water

1 $1/2$ tablespoons canola oil

1 $1/2$ tablespoons honey

1 $1/2$ teaspoons salt

1 $1/4$ cups (6.8 ounces) whole wheat flour

1 $1/2$ cups (7.8 ounces) unbleached flour

2 teaspoons active dry yeast

1. Put the ingredients in the bread pan in the order listed, or in the reverse order if the manual for your machine calls for dry ingredients first and liquids last. Select the Dough Cycle. Press Start.

2. When the cycle is complete, remove the dough and cut into 10 (1-pound recipe) or 16 (1 $1/2$-pound recipe) strips.

3. Roll each strip into a rope and shape ropes into pretzels. (See diagram.) Cover and let rise in a warm, draft-free place for about 45 minutes.

4. Bring 2 quarts of water with 4 teaspoons baking soda to a boil, then turn down heat to maintain a light simmer. Gently place each pretzel in the water with a slotted spoon. It is easiest to do each pretzel separately. Leave pretzels in the water approximately 1 minute, turning once.

5. Remove the pretzels and place on a lightly oiled baking pan. Sprinkle with coarse salt, poppy seeds, or sesame seeds, if desired.

6. Bake at 475°F. for 12 minutes.

Nutrient Analysis per serving: 1 pretzel

Calories: 103   *Fat: 2*

Carbohydrates: 19   *Fiber: 2*

Protein: 3

Braided Breads

Braided egg breads have been a part of the Jewish and Orthodox Christian traditions for hundreds of years. The two most popular shapes are a straight braid and a braid that forms a ring. Perhaps the most popular of all braided egg breads is the classic Jewish Challah. Devout Jewish women prepare this rich egg bread each Friday as an act of meditation in preparation for the Sabbath. Orthodox Christians prepare a braided egg loaf in the shape of a crown during Easter to commemorate the rebirth of Christ. They decorate the braid by pressing hard-boiled colored eggs into the dough before baking.

Basic Braided Loaf

A beautiful addition to any dinner party or holiday meal. You'll start a family tradition with this.

1-pound loaf (8 – 10 servings):

3/4 cup water
1 tablespoon canola oil
1 tablespoon honey
1 teaspoon salt
3/4 cup (4.1 ounces) whole wheat flour
1 cup (5.2 ounces) unbleached flour
1 1/2 teaspoons active dry yeast

1 1/2-pound loaf (12 – 14 servings):

1 1/8 cups water
1 1/2 tablespoons canola oil
1 1/2 tablespoons honey
1 1/2 teaspoons salt
1 1/4 cups (6.8 ounces) whole wheat flour
1 1/2 cups (7.8 ounces) unbleached flour
2 teaspoons active dry yeast

1. Put the ingredients in the bread pan in the order listed, or in the reverse order if the manual for your machine calls for dry ingredients first and liquids last. Select the Dough Cycle. Press Start.

2. When the cycle is complete, remove dough and place on a floured surface. Divide dough into three pieces and form strands approximately 9 to 12 inches long.

3. Pinch ropes together at one end and start forming a braid by weaving strands into each other. When braid is formed, pinch together at the bottom to secure the braid.

4. Place the braid on a lightly oiled baking sheet. Cover and let rise in a warm, draft-free place for about 45 minutes or until doubled in size.

5. Before baking, you may want to brush braided loaf with egg substitute or oil and sprinkle with sesame or poppy seeds. Bake at 375°F for 20 to 25 minutes.

Nutrient Analysis per Serving:
Calories: 138   *Fat: 2*
Carbohydrates: 25   *Fiber: 2*
Protein: 4

Whole Wheat Crescent Rolls

These will be in demand at every meal!

1-pound loaf (8 – 10 servings):

$3/4$ cup water
1 tablespoon canola oil
1 $1/2$ tablespoons honey
1 teaspoon salt
$3/4$ cup (4.1 ounces) whole wheat flour
1 cup (5.2 ounces) unbleached flour
2 tablespoons powdered whey
1 $1/2$ teaspoons active dry yeast
2 tablespoons egg substitute (reserve for brushing)

1 $1/2$-pound loaf (12 – 14 servings):

1 cup plus 2 tablespoons water
1 $1/2$ tablespoons canola oil
2 tablespoons honey
1 $1/2$ teaspoons salt
1 $1/4$ cups (6.8 ounces) whole wheat flour
1 $1/2$ cups (7.8 ounces) unbleached flour
3 tablespoons powdered whey
2 teaspoons active dry yeast
$1/4$ cup egg substitute (reserve for brushing)

1. Put the ingredients into the bread pan in the order listed, or in the reverse order if the manual for your machine calls for dry ingredients first and liquids last. Select Dough cycle. Press Start.

2. When cycle is finished, remove the dough and place in a lightly oiled bowl. Cover the bowl and let sit in a warm, draft-free place for 20 to 30 minutes.

3. Remove dough from bowl and cut into 10 to 12 (1-pound recipe) or 14 to 16 (1 $1/2$ -pound recipe) portions. Roll each portion into a smooth ball.

4. Cover the balls with a cloth and let them sit for 15 minutes.

5. When ready, form each ball of dough into a cone. Roll each cone until flat. One end will be wider.

6. Roll each cone from the wider side to the narrower side (see diagram).

(recipe continued)

7. Place all of the rolls, with the seam sides down, on a lightly oiled baking pan.

8. Spray each roll lightly with water and let them sit in a warm, draft-free place for 30 to 40 minutes until they almost double in size.

9. Brush rolls with egg substitute and bake in a preheated oven at 350°F for 10 to 15 minutes.

Nutrient Analysis per Serving:
Calories: 131
Carbohydrates: 25
Protein: 4
Fat: 2
Fiber: 3

Glossary

Amaranth A broad-leafed plant with multiple seed heads that is especially high in protein, fiber, and other nutrients. When used as a grain dish, cold cereal, or incorporated into muffins and breads, amaranth is an excellent protein complement to beans and other grains.

Barley A nutritious grain that is easy to digest and useful in stews and soups. A sweet additional flour in bread dough. Pearled barley, round and white, loses most of its original vitamins and minerals during milling. Hulled barley, which is less refined, is an excellent source of B vitamins and several minerals; it also contains a substance which inhibits the production of cholesterol.

Bran The outer covering of whole grains, composed of cellulose (an indigestible plant fiber) and major portions of the grain's protein, vitamins, and minerals. By increasing the bulk of feces and stimulating elimination, bran serves as an excellent laxative.

Buckwheat Not a true grain, though nutritionally similar to cereal grains. Toasted buckwheat grits are known as kasha.

Canola Oil The oil of selectively bred rapeseed plants. Contains an impressive balance between monounsaturated and polyunsaturated fatty acids (the monounsaturateds make it stable and less likely to go rancid). Canola oil also boasts the lowest percentage of saturated fat of any commercial cooking oil, making canola a useful oil in a healthy heart diet. The oil's name was changed from rapeseed oil to canola oil (a take off on "Canadian oil") as a marketing strategy, since the major growers of rapeseed are in Canada.

Carob Roasted and ground fruit pods from a Mediterranean evergreen tree. The tree is used ornamentally along city streets as well as commercially grown. Carob is a healthy alternative to chocolate because it is lower in fat, does not contain caffeine or theobromine (stimulants found in cocoa), and is less bitter than chocolate and so needs less sweetener.

Cornmeal Corn is a grain, not a vegetable as commonly assumed. Whole cornmeal is made from coarsely ground whole corn. Contains both the outer hull and germ of the grain. Whole cornmeal is superior in taste and nutritional value to degerminated cornmeal, which has had its fibrous hull and nutritious germ removed. Bolted cornmeal retains the fiber but not the germ.

Cracked Wheat Also known as bulgar. Made by crushing, toasting, and parboiling wheat berries. Used in cooked cereals, breads, soups, and casseroles.

Egg Substitute A commercially prepared alternative to eggs for those who wish to avoid the cholesterol found in egg yolks or for those who wish to avoid consuming animal products. Egg substitutes are available in liquid or powder forms. Liquid egg substitutes are stored in the refrigerator section of supermarkets and are composed of egg whites, vegetable oils, thickeners, synthetic nutrients, and coloring agents to enhance appeal. Powdered egg substitutes are typically found in natural food stores, and are made from tapioca, potato starch, calcium carbonate, and cellulose. A mere $1/4$ cup of liquid egg substitute equals one large egg; 4 tablespoons of powdered substitute equals 1 large egg. If you wish to use the timer feature on your bread machine, be certain to use powdered egg substitutes. Both fresh eggs and liquid egg substitutes spoil quickly unless refrigerated.

Fiber An indigestible part of the structure of food. There are two types of fiber, soluble and insoluble. Soluble fiber, found in apples, oats, and rice, binds with substances like cholesterol and bile acids to speed their transit through the intestine and reduce the risk of colon cancer and gallstones, among other medical conditions. Insoluble fiber, found in whole grains, potatoes, and beans, contributes bulk to the stools, acting like a broom to sweep out the stool and prevent diverticulosis and constipation.

Flax An annual with seeds that contains a rich supply of omega-3 fatty acids, which are used by the body in a number of important ways to protect against heart disease, cancer, and other degenerative diseases. Flaxseed oil must be purchased in opaque containers and stored in the refrigerator because it easily spoils when exposed to light.

Fructose A common sweetener used in baking. Appears naturally in fruits, honey, and other foods. Commercial fructose is either crystalline (made from refined cane and beet sugar) or liquid (refined corn syrup). Fructose is much sweeter than other sugars, so much less is needed in recipes. In addition, fructose is metabolized more slowly and by a different biochemical pathway than sucrose (table sugar), so it is recommended as an alternative to sugar for people with diabetes.

Ginger A rhizome, or underground stem, of the ginger plant. Its strong, tangy taste is popular in sauces and desserts. It has proven useful in relieving the nausea of motion sickness and the morning sickness of early pregnancy.

Gluten A plant protein found primarily in wheat. Gluten enables dough to capture the carbon dioxide escaping from the yeast's fermentation process, which causes bread to rise and maintain its light texture.

Granola A tasty snack that combines a variety of grains, nuts, seeds, and a small amount of oil and sweetener.

Honey Created by bees from flower nectar, honey is both a favorite sweetener and a useful antiseptic. It must not be given to infants under the age of one, because it sometimes carries spores of bacterial botulism, which can form a potentially deadly toxin in the baby's (but not in older children's or adults') intestines.

Kamut An ancient ancestor of modern wheat. Can be eaten by people who are allergic to wheat. Kamut has a buttery flavor.

Maple Syrup A sweetener made from the sap of sugar maple trees, maple syrup containing about 50 calories per tablespoon along with some calcium and potassium. Pure maple syrup is expensive but delicious. Inexpensive brands often contain very little true maple syrup, and high amounts of corn syrup, sugar, honey, molasses, fruit juice, coloring, chemicals, and artificial flavors. Keep pure maple syrup in the refrigerator to prevent mold or fermentation.

Millet A yellow, round grain that is a staple in other parts of the world but is mostly ignored in the United States. Gluten-free, millet is a tasty and nutritious alternative to those sensitive to wheat. It is easy to digest and high in iron and protein.

Molasses A by-product of white sugar production. Used as a sweetener and darkening agent. Blackstrap molasses is the most concentrated grade of molasses, the most flavorful, and the most nutritious (particularly high in iron). The lighter grades have only up to half the iron of blackstrap molasses but still contain impressive amounts of essential minerals.

Oats A cereal grass available rolled (for oatmeal), flaked, steel-cut, or as groats. A good source of vitamin B complex and fiber. In closed containers, oats have a shelf-life measured in years. Because oats are low in gluten, they must be paired with wheat or gluten flour for bread baking.

Oat Bran Oat bran is the outer covering of the oat grain and has been found to efficiently bind cholesterol and thereby help remove it from the body through the intestines.

Pumpernickel A sourdough bread made from unsifted rye flour and colored with molasses, coffee, postum, carob, or caramel coloring.

Quinoa Pronounced "Keen-wa." Provides nearly twice the protein and greater quantities of other nutrients than most grains, yet cooks in 20 minutes or less. Low in gluten, it must be combined with wheat flour in bread making.

Rye A low-gluten grain with a strong flavor. Mixes well with other grains in breads and granola.

Soy Milk Composed of cooked soybeans and therefore completely free of lactose and cholesterol. Comparable to cow's milk in calories, protein, fat, and sodium content. May contain calcium caseinate, a derivative of milk. Nevertheless, soy milk is useful for people who are lactose intolerant or who are avoiding cholesterol.

Spelt An easily digested whole grain that tastes similar to wheat. Can be consumed by people allergic to wheat.

Sucanat™ A natural sweetener distilled from organically grown sugar cane. Free of chemical residues, additives, preservatives, or other artificial ingredients. May be substituted for refined sugar in recipes of all sorts.

Tofu Also called bean curd. A protein-rich food that is particularly popular in Asian countries. Tofu is created from the mixture of soybeans, water, and a mineral coagulant. Tofu's low calories and mild taste make it an ideal addition to strong-tasting casseroles, stir-fries, or party dips. It also can be used as a cheese alternative. Highly perishable, tofu must be kept in a water bath that is changed daily. Fresh tofu must remain refrigerated.

Triticale A cross between wheat and rye. Contains more protein than wheat but has a lower gluten content. Found in natural foodstores. Use up to two-thirds triticale to one-third wheat in baking.

Wheat Germ The growth center of the wheat kernel. Contains the wheat's richest store of nutrients.

Whey The water and milk solids that remain after the curd is removed in cheese making. An easily digested, nutritious source of protein and a thickening agent in baked goods and sauces. Helps keep breads moist but firm.

Whole Wheat On packaging, the words *wheat flour* is a synonym for refined wheat that has had is major nutrients milled away. A bread that is truly "whole wheat" will have the word *whole* or *100% whole wheat* on the label.

Yeast Tiny, one-celled fungi that feed on sugars in bread dough, multiply, and give off carbon dioxide as a byproduct of their growth and activity. The carbon dioxide is caught in gluten strands of the dough, causing bread to rise as it bakes. Active yeast is available in solid cakes or dry powder.

Index

199

International Conversion Chart

These are not exact equivalents; they've been slightly rounded to make measuring easier.

CUP MEASUREMENTS

AMERICAN	IMPERIAL	METRIC	AUSTRALIAN
1/4 cup (2 oz.)	2 fl. oz.	60 ml	2 Tablespoons
1/3 cup (3 oz)	2 fl. oz.	84 ml	1/4 cup
1/2 cup (4 oz.)	4 fl. oz.	125 ml	1/3 cup
2/3 cup (5 oz.)	5 fl. oz.	170 ml	1/2 cup
3/4 cup (6 oz.)	6 fl. oz.	185 ml	2/3 cup
1 cup (8 oz.)	8 fl. oz.	250 ml	3/4 cup

SPOON MEASUREMENTS

AMERICAN	METRIC
1/4 teaspoon	1ml
1/2 teaspoon	2 ml
1 teaspoon	5 ml
1 tablespoon	15 ml

OVEN TEMPERATURES

FARENHEIT	CENTIGRADE
250	120
300	150
325	160
350	180
375	190
400	200
450	230